FEAR, UNREST AND ANXIETY OF ADOLESCENTS

FEAR, UNREST
AND
ANXIETY OF ADOLESCENTS

DR. T. ROMALA RAYALU
Dept. of Human Development and Family Studies,
College of Home Sciences,
Hyderabad- 500 004.

Discovery Publishing House
New Delhi-110 002

First Published-1998

Reprinted: 2013

ISBN 81-7141-436-2

Published by:
DISCOVERY PUBLISHING HOUSE
4831/24, Ansari Road, Prahlad Street,
Daryaganj, New Delhi-110 002 (*INDIA*)
Phone: 3279245
Fax: 91-11-3253475

Printed at: Dynamic printers, Delhi

PREFACE

The curriculum which does not consider the level of pupils emotional development cannot be effective in attaining goals of education. The Philosophers emphasize the need of 'Abhaya' (fearlessness) for the man to be risen to an illumined consciousness from the intellectual plane. The chief objective of the education should be not merely the academic achievements, but also the development of the total personality. It is the function of education to eliminate fear, to see that pupils do not become mechanical at the same time to give the pupils the knowledge.

This book is based on fears of Adolescents-A comparative study of fears of Indian and British adolescents. A science attempt was made to study the extent and intensity of fears of adolescent boys and girls in cross-cultural context.

Systematic studies of the fears of adolescents are saprisimply scarce in the research literature. Little is known about the fears of adolescents what is appraised as threatning depends upon the physical, social and cultural environment in which individuals grow up and live. A sample of 1064 adolescents were drawn from various schools of India and United Kingdom. The present investigation is a contribution to this area of knowledge by gathering information about fears of normal adolescents in relation to the variables of age, sex and nationality, utilying a fear survey schedule. The quantitative, and qualitative characteristics of reported fears have been assessed in terms of the frequency, and degree of intensity with recordings were made. This book provides relevant information to parent teachers, councellors, educationists, psychologists, social workers and specialists in Human Development and Family Studies and serve as valuable source material for consultation.

I am greatly indebited to Dr. J. H. Bounber, senior lecturer, Dept. of education Queens University of Belfast, United Kingdom and Dr. K. Ramachandra Reddy, professor, psychology department, Osmania University, Hyderabad for there guidance and cooperation. My special thanks are due to all adolescents who participated in this study.

Author

ACKNOWLEDGEMENT

I am grateful to Dr. K. R. Reddy, professor of psychology, Osmania University, for his guidance in preparing this book. I am indicated to Dr. J. H. Bamber, Senior lecturer, Queen's University of Belfast, United Kingdom for his help from inception of this study.

My heartful thanks are due to Dr. E. G. Parameswaran, Dean of Education, Osmania University, Dr. M. Malla Reddy, Director, SERT for their suggestions and help given in carrying out this investigation.

I thank all the principals, teaching staff and students of the schools selected for the study in Northern Ireland, U.K. and Hyderabad, India who have given their cooperation in collecting data for this study.

I express my gratitude to Andhra Pradesh Agricultural University and Dean Dr. (Mrs.) Geervani, Faculty of Home Science for granting me leave to complete this study.

My sincere thanks are due to Discovery Publishing House who made it possible to bring this manuscript on the book form. I am extremely grateful to them for this cooperation and keep intent.

T. Romala Royalu.

Contents

1
Introduction

Systematic studies of the fears of adolescents are surprisingly scarce in the research literature. There are grounds for maintaining that information about the fears of adolescents is of value and has a practical relevance. Lapouse and Monk (1959) and Maurer (1965) have justified the study of human fears on the grounds that psychistric judgements require the backing of normative studies.

From the standpoint of behavioural dynamics, there is the observation by Feshback and Feshback (1963) that frightened individuals tend to distort their judgements of other people. Answers from an educational standpoint can be derived from the work of Weinstein and Fantini (1968), that a relevant curriculum requires to touch upon the learner's effective concerns. The curriculum which does not consider the level of pupils emotional development cannot be effective in attaining goals of education. The Hindu philosophers also emphasize the need of 'Abhaya' (fearlessness) for the man to be risen to an illumined consciousness from the intellectual plane. The intellect must grow to such an extent whereby it becomes illunised and free from fear. The freedom from fear is acquired by deepening the awareness of self and growing into a larger world. Similarly, Angelino Dollins and Mech (1956) point to the role of fears on the education of the whole child. The chief objective of the education should be not merely the academic achievements, but also the development of the total personality. Krishnamurthy Jiddu (1974) regards that it is the function of education to eliminate fear as it prevents the flowering of the mind and the flowering of goodness in man. He argues that fear is the essence of authority and obedience. When the brain is conforming to a pattern of obedience, is no longer capable of thinking simply and directly.

The first great virtue derived from education is fearlessness. Knowledge destroys fear. Physical science destroys fear proceeding from external world. Spiritual science destroys fears proceeding from within. Fear is the great enemy of the moral life. Fearlessness comes from knowledge of the laws governing the world. Swami Vivekananada says that where there is no fear, there will be no superstition. Learning only comes into being when there is no fear and when there is no authority. When there is fear, learning is ceased. So it is the function of education to eliminate fear, to see that the pupils do not become mechanical and at the same time to give the pupils the knowledge.

The individual cannot learn unless he is free from fear, individuals learning is blocked if he is under the influence of fear. A frightened individual cannot judge and reason out things clearly and effectively. His attention and concentration are affected and his state of mind would be confused. The goals of education cannot be achieved with the pupils who are not free from fear. Therefore it should be the function of education to eliminate fear in pupils to make them think constructively and act independently without fear.

According to Albert camus, we live in a 'Century of fear'. If we live in a 'Century of fear' and anxiety is the central problem of large areas of psychological theory, how much do we know about the fears of normal children and adolescents ? In 1949 Hurlock wrote that little was known about the fears of adolescents, while Barecz writing in 1968, stated that, the results of studies of fears in normal children were not very gratifying. He went on to add that 'very little is known about the qualitative characteristics of fears of normal children relative to age and other important variables.

What is appraised as threatening depends upon the physical, social and cultural environment in which individuals grow up and live. What is fear provoking in one culture with its specifically characteristics is not necessarily fear provoking in another culture with other characteristics. Therefore cross-cultural research on fear would seem to provide an excellent approach for establishing general laws about human experience and behaviour.

The present investigation has attempted to make a contribution to this area of knowledge by gathering information about the fears of normal adolescents in relation to the variables of age, sex and nationality (culture) utilizing a fear survey schedule. The quantitative and qualitative characteristics of reported fears have been assessed in terms of the frequency and degree of intensity with which recordings were made.

Concepts of Fear

The word fear comes from the Old English 'fear' for sudden calamity or danger and was later used to describe emotion of uneasiness caused by the sense of impending danger. In Medieval English it continued to denote a state of alarm or dread and does so still today.

Fear is physiological arousal for which an individual has no immediate explanation. (Schachter & Singer 1962). The word 'fear' would apply to states described by the second proposition *i.e.*, a completely appropriate explanation is offered for the state of physiological arousal. Whether a state of physiological arousal is related to proposition, this fear as experienced by the individual is determined according to whether he records as having the fear a little, a fair amount, much or very much. One or two depends upon the individuals ability to explain and 'label' this state. Fears such as growing old, not every getting married, of the next war, of being illegitimate child of somebody, your dislikes may be real but do not usually, have distinctive and clear-out physical accompaniments tied to them. Iyard and Tomkins (1966) pointed out the object or "explanation" attached to the state of fear depends upon accurate perception, and correct identification.

Fear refers to feelings of apprehension about tangible and predominantly realistic dangers. (J. Rachman, 1978). It is one of the primitive, violent and usually crippling emotions, marked by extensive bodily changes and by behaviour of the flight or concealment character (Drever, 1954). Fear includes cognitive elements in some of its basic uses of the term. The concept of fear in relation to its objects is something which human learn—What it means to be afraid is identified, both in ourselves and others, and in observing what people do in association with 'dangerous—threatening' objects.

Fear is used exclusively for the attitude toward feel dangers threatening from external sources and later exclusively for reactions, to threats located within the mind, due to clashes between drives and internal opposing forces, while fears, however strong they are, do not develop into phobias, anxiety does so under certain conditions (Anna Freud, 1977).

Fear is a normal response to active or imagined threat in higher animals and comprises an outer behavioural expression, an inner feeling and accompanying physiological changers (Landis, 1964).

Fear has occupied a prominent place in most discussions of emotions. It have been described as the 'Central problem of neurosis' (Freud, 1936). It's importance is probably related to the fact that "since stressing and potentially destructive conditions far outnumber and outweigh the constructive conditions, readiness for avoidance reaction generally dominates readiness for acquisitive action (Kempf. 1958).

Logical analysis made us derive different significant ways of observing the concept of fear. Fear can be groundless such as it would be unreasonable to fear that the building in which one is writing an article is about to collapse and crush one to death if all the evidence suggests it is structurally sound, no real possibility of an earthquake, and adequately searched for the bombs of terrorists, etc. Fears are irrational in the kind in which the person agrees that there is no danger—and believes this—but remains afraid. One might be afraid of harmless grass—snakes or loads, having perhaps acquired a sort of conditioned fear to such harmless objects in childhood. Fears may be superstitious also. A man may feel apprehensive if a black cat crosses his path or he 'reads' disaster in a pack of cards. Neurotic fears are those in which the object of fear is an inappropriate one. To be afraid ofbeing in an open space, or ofbeing at the top of the tower with high railings, or of birds or beetles is to be afraid of what does not threaten one or include any real danger. It is unreasonable to be afraid when the object is an appropriate object of fear but when one's reaction is exaggerated or excessive. It is reasonable to be afraid of cobra but unreasonable to scream and faint when one sees one on a film or when it is safely behind glass in a zoo.

The concept of 'fear' is more complex in meaning than appears at first attempts at definition. 'Fear' as a concept means a complex interaction between organism and environment resulting in certain consequences.

Behaviour, in fear is related to the background of events in which we are alert and intelligently aware. A civilian caught up in a battle area, under the influence of fear, may take a flight or hide. Fear may be aroused due to dependence on wants and needs that are artificial or contingent upon what we have learned to value. On how we construe certain human activities and employments and relationships. Thus a politician may genuinely fear another fellow members of his political party as a threat to his ambitions of becoming a leader or minister.

Anthony Kenny's (1963) analysis suggests that fears as a concept is identified by the use of three types of criteria :

(1) Circumstances of threat in the environment;
(2) Physical symptoms;
(3) Avoidance behaviour resulting from some perception of 'Objects' of fear;

Shakespeare said, "of all the bad passions fear is most accused".

Conceptual analysis of 'fear' suggests that the term refers to a complex situation of 'action related to context': environmental circumstances, the agent's appraisal of them, states and predispositions of the agent, his action in relation to the object all being involved.

Fear and Anxiety

It is a curious fact that when we use concepts like fear or anxiety we can easily relate them to our personal experiences; we know what it is like to be afraid of or anxious. Obvious definitions, *e.g.* that fear refers to a present situation, while anxiety refers to a future or past state, do not take very far. Philosophers and Psychologists alike attempted to describe and explain fear and anxiety but never found their job all that easy.

Drever (1952) in "A Dictionary of Psychology" provides the following definitions:

1. **Fear:** One of the primitives, violent and usually crippling emotions, marked by extensive bodily changes, and by behaviour of the flight or concealment character.
2. **Anxiety:** A chronic complex emotional state with apprehensive or dread as its most prominent component; characteristic of various nervous and mental disorders.

We find lack of clarity when we examine the definitions given by Drever.

'Fear' and 'anxiety' both have an emotional element. The difference between the two would seem to lie in the fact that 'fear' produces 'flight or concealment behaviour', whereas 'anxiety' does not.

Fear is specific reaction and anxiety involves fear or more of the fundamental emotions, negative (distress, shame, anger etc.) or positive (interest, excitement etc.).

Anxiety is pervasive and profound phenomenon. Be it healthy or non-healthy, all persons suffer from anxiety or experience anxiety. In psychiatric illness particularly there is one thing in common and that is anxiety.

Por Hoch (1950) pointed out the central problem concerned the contradiction inherent in anxiety as both an adaptive or destructive process. As a signal, it provides a useful warning of danger, but it is itself, can become more dangerous than the danger it warns of.

Liddell (1950) stated that he believed that anxiety accompanies intellectual activity as its shadow and that the more we know of the nature of anxiety the more we know intellect, intellect and its shadow anxiety are products of man's social intercourse.

There are writers whose equate fear with anxiety, and there are those who attempt to differentiate between them. An example of equating the terms 'fear' and 'anxiety' is found in Joseph Wolpe and Sandor Rado's descriptions. Wolpe (1958) states. The word 'anxiety' is used ... Synonymously with fear'. There is no reason to think that there is any physiological difference between the fear aroused by a stimulus that is associated with/an objective threat *e.g.* a rattlesnake, and fear that is unadaptive, aroused, *e.g.* by kitten".

Wolpe's case rests on the physiological similarity between two states. But other claim that the two states can be distinguished on physiological basis. Lief (1967) Wolff & Wolff (1947) are of the view that fear and anxiety are different on physiological grounds.

Rado (1964) equates the terms 'fear' and 'anxiety' since they both were derived from the Latin root 'Augustia'. Rado further argues "In order to aid clear thinking we ought to discard this unhappy word (*i.e.* anxiety) from our technical language and revert to the exclusive use of the word fear". Dixon, de Mouchaux and Sandler (1957) state that the distinction of fear and anxiety and was made in psychoanalytical theory.

In order to specify fear and anxiety it is often necessary to refer to its object. The writings of English and Pearson (1965), Jersild (1960) and Despert (1946) illustrate differences based on the objectivity of what is feared.

Differentiation of fear is made with fear referring to an immediate objective threat while anxiety seems to be an anticipated subjective danger. English and Pearson (1965) while nothing that both fear and anxiety have similar functions *i.e.* both are signals to the person that he is in some serious danger, point out that "the actual cause of neurotic anxiety is not conscious and we usually do not know why we fell the discomfort from it". According to Jersild (1960)" the main distinction that has been made between fear and anxiety is that fear is a response to an objective danger, while anxiety is wholly or in large part a response to a subjective danger and also notes "serval characteristics of 'fear' that might indicate the existence of anxiety".

From the analysis of Jerslid and Despert it can be concluded that fears reflect objective threats while in other cases fears objectify anxiety.

The quotings of Worslay (1961) and May (1950) illustrate that fear is an outcrop of anxiety. Worsley states "Anxiety is the primary mental emotion. Fear is a by-product of it (*i.e.* fear is really anxiety bound to an object or idea)". May notes that "anxiety is a diffuse apprehension, and (that) the central difference between fear and anxiety is that fear is a reaction to a specific danger while anxiety is unspecified, 'Vague', 'objectless'." May also distinguished between "normal" and "neurotic" anxiety, normal anxiety being used "in the form of what Fraud termed 'objective anxiety' ". He stated the relation between anxiety to fear and neurotic anxiety to neurotic fear is that "anxiety is the basic, underlying reaction—the generic term; and fear is the expression of the same capacity in its specific, objectivated form".

May (1950) observed that not only to 'fear' and 'anxiety' vary in their degree of specificity, they also differ in the sequence of maturation.

According to Lewis (1967) the word anxiety is used habitually to refer to an emotional state with the subjectively experienced quality of fear or a closely related emotion.

The nature and origin of anxiety are obscure, the nature and origin of fear are simple and readily intelligible.

Sullivan (1956) clarifies the distinction between fear and anxiety. Fear is a generally found, self protective reaction to a painful or novel situation; anxiety on the other hand, is a product of education.

Fear is used exclusively for the attitude toward real dangers threatening from external sources and anxiety, exclusively for reaction to threats located within the mind, due to clashes between drives and internal opposing forces.

The literature reveals considerable ambiguity in regard to anxiety and fear because of a frequent tendency to use these terms in a synonymous manner, or the two are confused. Anxiety and fear are not synonymous but are closely related to the extent where one emotion quickly or subsequently follows perception of the other regardless of whether the experienced anxiety is based on the fear situation of earlier experience or the perceived fear due to recurring anxiety.

Fear and Phobia

Rachman (1968) defines 'Phobias' as ".......... persistent, excessive fear reactions, maladaptive conditioned responses which have been acquired in a painful or excessively frightening situation".

From Rachman's definition the object of phobia seems to be not normally regarded as being objectively threatening and the reaction is excessive.

Hipocrates writings contain two of the earliest clinical descriptions of man who feared that which need not be feared. Errera (1962) provides a comprehensive definition of the term, as a persisting fear of an object or of an idea which does not ordinarily justify fear". Marks (1966) offers a definition with more specific details: "Phobias are a special kind of fear *i.e.* a persistent, excessive fear attached to an object or situation which objectively is not a significant source of danger. A phobia can thus be defined as a special form of fear which (1) is out of proportion to the demands of the situation; (2) cannot be explained or reasoned away; (3) is beyond voluntary control; (4) leads to avoidance of the feared situation".

Phobia can be analysed into three components: (1) subjective; (2) autonomic; and (3) motor. The subjective aspect of phobic response is experienced by the person as an alarming feeling of intense fear tension or full panic and is experienced in variety of ways. Some report, they feel as if they are dying, others feel they are suffocating or they are going to faint or collapse.

The motor response to usually one of flight but patients become inert or "frozen" and feel too weak to move. The common phobias are claustrophobia, agoraphobia, acrophobia, animal phobias, interpersonal phobias, death-disease, injury phobias, sexual phobias.

A Theory of Phobias

(1) Phobias are learned responses.

(2) Stimulus develop phobic qualities when they are associated temporally and spatially with a fear producing state of affairs.

(3) Neutral stimuli which are of relevance are more likely to develop phobic qualities than week or irrelevant stimuli.

(4) Repetition of the association between the fear situation and the new phobic stimuli which strengthen the phobia.

(5) Associations between high-intensity fear situations or neutral stimuli are more likely to produce phobic reactions.

(6) Generalization from the original phobic stimulus to stimuli of a similar nature will occur.

(7) Noxious experiences under conditions of excessive confinement are more likely to produce phobic reactions.

(8) Responses which reduces the fear drive are reinforced (*e.g.* avoidance).

(9) Phobic reactions can be acquired vicariously.

An individual can overcome a fear by help in normal life whereas the phobic needs therapy.

The three terms 'Anxiety', 'Fear' and 'Phobia' can be differentiated by the degree of emotion as mild, moderate and excessive.

Anxiety can result in both fear and phobia. Fear which is unrelated to the real situation leads to phobia. Fear which is expressive as a reflexive action will quite often be followed by anxiety (not necessarily always).

As it can be seen from above discussion Fear encompasses a very large area and viewed differently by different people particularly by different age groups. The sources of fear are also many and divergent at times it become highly subjective. Although there is an universality about fear, the subjective experience of source and intensity are numerous and divergent. Hence there is a need for an operational definition of fear for the purpose of this investigation. The following operational definition has been therefore postulated: *The positive reaction an individual makes to a verbal stimulus on a questionnaire when he is asked to pick out those items which he thinks he might find frightening or unpleasant. A strength of this fear, as experienced by the individual, is determined according to whether he records as having the fear a little, a fair amount, much or very much.*

Types of Fears

Innate and Acquired

Innate elements are those which appear early in life before there has been significant experience.

Fear is an innate emotional response in higher animals which has obvious survival value. This emotional response varies in strength in two ways, (1) regardless of situation the overall fearfulness of an individual varies from one individual to individual. (2) regardless of individuals, some situations are more feared than others and this variation may also be species specific.

Many of Valentine's (1950) arguments in support of the view that many fears have an innate elements are infact criticism of Watson's (1913) view that fears are conditioned responses.

According to Watson (1913) the innate stimuli for fear can be limited to

(a) hearing a sudden loud noise;
(b) loss of support;
(c) experiencing pain;
(d) sudden movements made by others.

Hebb (1946) concluded on Valentine's follow-up of Watson's experiment that it is easy to condition fear of certain things and hard to condition with some others, and thus demonstrating the existence of emotional susceptibilities which are the basis of Spontaneous fears. Valentine's findings were also confirmed in a study conducted by

Bergman (1934).

Two other areas of fear which appear to have strong claims to be regarded as innate are fear of heights and fear of strangers. Gibson and Walk (1960) demonstrated fear of height in their phenomena of visual cliff.

All other fears which are resultant of human experience are said to be acquired in nature.

Valentine (1950) investigated some of the fears in children such as fear of rain, fear of the very strange and to fear live and moving things.

Maturational

Hebb discusses about the development of fear of stranger. Maturation of this fear depends on prior learning to recognize familiar individuals. This was proved by him in the experiments on Chimpanzees. Both Valentine (1950), Jersild and Holmes (1953) support the idea that fear of dark arise at about 2 years and continue to grow in intensity until age of 5 years in human beings.

Jones and Jones (1928) demonstrated that fear of snakes is maturational in that a definite fear only emerges around the age of 4 years.

Work of Spitz (1965), Morgan and Riccuti (1967) have shown that fear of strangers begins to appear between 6 and 3 months in the child increases to maximum by 12 months and continues throughout the second year of life, though alterable through experience, this fear is universal at a particular age.

Marks and Gelder (1966) attempted to account for their finding regarding the early onset of animal phobias by postulating the concept of a facilitatory period in human during which avoidance responses could be acquired to limited class of objects much more readily than at other ages. The concepts of a facilitatory period would imply that maturation partly determines which environmental stimuli produce fear responses at different ages. Valentine himself stressed the role of maturation in which connection and described the evidence he collected about one of his children.

Anna Freud (1970) has traced a certain developmental chronology in the emergence of fears :

(1) Archaic (*i.e.*, fears of darkness, noise, strangers, solitude etc.);

(2) Separation fears (*viz.*, fears of annihilation, starvation, loneliness, helplessness etc.);

(3) Fears of loss of love (*viz.*, fears of punishment, rejection, desertion, earthquakes, thunder storms, death etc.);

(4) Castration Fears (*viz.*, fears of operations, mutilation, doctors, dentists, illness, poverty, robbers, witches, ghosts etc.);

(5) Fears of social disgrace.

Ethologists studied the fear of conspecifies on 'Sign—Stimuli'. Tinbergen's (1951) experiment on ethological fish has shown that sign stimuli is innate.

Bowlby (1944) stressed the fear of being separated unwillingly from an attachment figure at any phase of life cycle cease to be a puzzle and instead becomes classifiable as an instinctive response to one of the naturally occurring clues to an increased risk of danger.

Theories of Fear

Psychoanalytical

In Freud S. (1961) work "Inhibitions, Symptoms and Anxiety" fear is defined as : (a) "a special state of unpleasure with acts of discharge along particular paths"; (b) "a signal given by the ego in order to affect the unpleasure—pleasure agency"; (c) "an effective state and as such can, of course, only be felt by the ego". Thus for Freud, 'fear is ego-centered, it is an affective state with a characteristic response, and it acts as a signal to trigger off feelings of unpleasure. Fear arose originally, according to Freud, as a reaction to a state of danger and is reproduced whenever a state of that kind recurs.

The psychology of fear is further developed by Freud in his analysis of fear states. By a fear state he meant "the reproduction of some experience which contained the necessary conditions for an increase of excitation and discharge along particular paths, and that from this circumstance the unpleasure of fear receives its specific character. In man, birth provides a prototype experience of this kind and we are therefore inclined to regard fear-states as a reproduction of the trauma of birth". Thus, fear is not newly created in repression, it is reproduced as an affective state in accordance with an already existing anemic image (*i.e.* the psychological equivalent of a memory-trace).

With reference to psychoanalytical theory of fear the concept of neurotic fear should be made clear in particular. Discussion of neurotic fear requires mention of the concept of 'Symptom'. A symptom is a sign of, or a substitute for, an instinctual satisfaction which has remained in abeyance. It is a consequence of the process of repression which proceeds from the ego when the latter refuses to associate itself with an institutional cathexis aroused in the id.

Gero (1955) has argued that the displacement which takes place in symptom formation in phobias is a diphasic set of acts. The first phase consists of the potential release of impulses or drives (*i.e.* displacement). What is of importance about Gero's view is his suggestion that the two phases of the process do not have to follow each other slowly. Long stretches of time can elapse between the decisive repression and the displacement which results in a phobia. Thus phobias can first appear in adult life although childhood events have prepared the ground for them. The symptom originates when libidinal impulses are strong and when at the same time repression is increased.

The case history of little Hans illustrates the point that the human tendency to follow the line of least resistance and unimaginatively accept the first likely explanation for a given phenomenon which comes to hand. Though Stream (1967) interpretation might seem somewhat too speculative, the interpretations offered by Wolpe and Rachman (1963) and Rado. S (1964) are serious contenders, on the evidence available, to that offered by Freud.

Neuropsychological

An account of neuropsychological approach of fear is presented by Hebb in an article entitled "On the Nature of Fear" (1946). In his neuropsychological theory, Hebb designates the specific pattern of cellular activity throughout the thalamo-cortical system, at any point in time, as a "Phase". Each phase is determined by a neural interaction between the preceding phase and the concurrent afferent excitations. He also tells us: "The immediate source of fear is a disruption of a coordination, principally acquired, in the timing of cellular activities in the cerebrum. The disruption may be due to conflict, sensory deficit or constitutional charge. With disruption these at once occurs processes tending to restore the integration of cerebral activities; in fear these include either liminal or subliminal activation of processes determining avoidance. Optimally, avoidance tends towards completely averting the cerebeal disruption, and at this stage avoidance without fear would be said to occur". The disruption which leads to fear, as the quotation notes, can occur in several ways, of which Hebb details four. Disruption can also vary in degree so that a single mechanism of fear could, on different occasions, produce: perfectly coordinated flight; less coordinated avoidance, accompanied by trembling etc.; startle; the paralysis of terror.

Fears Due to 'Conflict'

Under this category Hebb includes fears induced by pain, fears of loud noises, fears of dead or mutilated bodies, and fears of strange persons and animals. About fears of pain and loud noises Hebb comments that they "appear to have a primitive disrupting action, not psychologically analyzable nor dependent on any previous experience".

Fears Due to 'Sensory Deficit'

These fears all have in common an absence of customary stimulation. Fear emerge when physical support is withdrawn because proprioceptive and pressure stimulation due to maintained position in space is practically always present. It is plausible to suppose that the afferent excitation from these sources would have an essential part in maintaining experientially organized or habitual, modes of cerebral action. A similar explanation can be given to account for fears induced by darkness and solitude being placed in this category.

Fears Due to 'Constitutional Disturbances and Maturation'

Nutritional disturbances such as pellagra can cause acute psychotic fears of friends and relations and of hallucinatory creatures. These fears cease dramatically upon the administration of nicotinic acid. Such fears illustrate the disruption caused to the orderly sequence of cerebral events by metabolic changes. Hebb suggests that endocrine factors might at times produce a similar effect, partly accounting for the increased shyness and emotional instability of adolescence. Maturation is sometimes thought of as being slow and gradual, but there is every likelihood that the endocrine spurt at adolescence (*viz.* Garrison) might well make a significant modification to cerebral organizations established by earlier experience.

Some confirmation of Hebb's view, that fear sterns from cerebral disruption provoked by difficulties relating to information processing or constitutional change, is to be found in the work done by Jones (1933) at an earlier period. That maturation plays an important role in determining the level of 'Preparedness operating on emotional behaviour was illustrated in an experiment conducted by Jones and Jones (1928). As a child develops, his intelligence innately matures, and his perception become enriched through experience. New things startle him because of his keener perception of the fact that they are new and unusual. Finally, fear arises when we know enough to recognize the potential danger in a situation but have not advanced to the point of complete comprehension and control of the changing situation.

Learning Approach

The work of Rachman (1968) Wolpe (1958) and Eysenck & Rachman, S. (1965) has contributed much to the learning theory approach of fear. Rachman points out that phobic disorders can best be regarded as conditioned fear reactions.

Origin of fears as proposed by Wolpe and Rachman in 1960 says that "Any neutral stimulus, simple or complex, that makes an impact on an individual at about the time that a fear reaction is evoked, acquires the ability to evoke fear subsequently. If the fear in the original conditioning situation was of high intensity, or if the conditioning is repeated a good many times, the conditioned fear will show the persistence that is characteristic of neurotic fear; and there will be generalization of fear reactions to stimuli resembling the conditioned stimulus".

The acquisition of fears by vicarious classical conditioning is discussed by Bandura (1965). As described by Bandura in the case of vicarious classical conditioning" the observer's vicariously elicited emotional responses become conditioned, through contiguous association, to formerly neutral stimuli". Vicarious classical conditioning seems a plausible way to account for such fears as those of snakes when it is known that the individual concerned has never had any direct aversive experience with reptiles.

Studies of normal classical conditioning have indicated the importance, for both acquisition and extinction. According to Bandura, degree of psychological stress experienced is also important in the acquisition and maintenance of vicariously acquired conditioned responses.

Berger and McGaugh (1965) argues that conditioning is not the mere substitution of a conditioned stimulus for an unconditioned stimulus since the conditions response is typically unlike the unconditioned response. The experiments on little Albert B, described by Watson and Rayner (1920) were designed to illustrate the method whereby the range of stimuli which can call out fear response is increased, from sharp noises and the sudden removal of support at birth, to the adult range of complexity.

English (1930) tried to establish fear response in two very young girl subjects, using a technique similar to that used by Watson and Rayner. It was found that over so many trials, conditioned response could not be established.

Despite the claims made by such writers as Eysenck and Rachman (1965). ("The classical demonstration of the development of phobia..."), these are grounds for questioning how far the above work can serve as a paradigm for accounting for the acquisition of fears in human beings.

In next chapter a review of research done in fears is presented starting from the year 1897 to 1989.

2

Review of Literature

Hall (1897) found fears of 'bodily harm', 'robbers' and 'death' increase beyond the 6th year; fear of 'dark' increases during pubescence with a decline in adulthood; Fear of 'ghosts', 'domestic animals' and of insects' increase until end of pubescence and fear of 'reptiles' increased with the age. He also found that females have a greater percentage of fears than males. He listed 10 most feared items upto age 23 years (*i.e.* Thunder, Lighting; reptiles; darkness; Strange persons; fire; death; disease; insects; wild animals; ghosts, water).

The case history of 'little hans' is a study in phobias by Freud (1909). While analyzing the development of phobia Freud said that the fear belonging to phobia would only emerge when its object is perceived.

Watson & Rayner (1920) proved that it is quite possible for one's experience to induce phobia. Their experiments on eleven month old infant called 'Little Albert' resulted in conditioning the fear and a phenomenon known as 'Stimulus Generalization'.

Jersild and Holmes (1935), noted 10 fears which increased with Age between birth and the 6th year. They wear, bodily harm, threat of injury, sings of fears in others, fears arising during dreams, robbers, kidnappers, death, dark (being alone in the dark), fear of imaginary creatures, abandonment by parents. Hall's finding that fear of 'reptiles' increased with age and fear of domestic animals and of 'insects' increased until the end of pubescence were not confirmed in the studies conducted by jersild and Holmes. The unique feature of Jersild and

Holmes experiments is age by age comparison using a given method of data collection at a particular point of time.

From Means (1936), study of Fears of 1000 College women enables us to draw a list of ten most feared items. They are, snakes, bulls, cancer, insane people, mad dogs, drunken men, wrecklers driving, death of loved ones, yellow jackets, burglars. Similarly, the ten most feared items from Hicks and Hayes (1938) study can be drawn as snakes, dogs, the dark, storms, accidents, high places, strange noises, being alone at home, burglars and the unknown.

Pratt (1945), in his study indicated that children studying in Grades. 5, 6, 7 and 8 had significantly greater mean number of fears than children in grades K,1, 2, 3 and 4; 75% of the fears reported were of animals; Girls listed a significantly greater number of fears than did boys and also, had greater percentage of fears of 'arthopods than boys.

Winker (1949) concluded that order children show a greater frequency of fears of bodily injury and younger children show fear of animals a great deal than do elder ones.

Angellno and Shedd (1953) designed a study to determine the shift in the content of fears as related to chronological age from 10 to 18 years. The findings reveal that at ages, 10, 11 and 12, there was a preponderance of fears connected with animals; at age 13 there was a shift to school connected content; fears related to political and economical interest begin to dominate at age 15 and increase upto age 18.

MoFarlen, Allen and Honzik (1954) found that specific fears declined with age, save for a 1 year spurt at age 11 for both boys and girls; girls showed significantly more fears than boys only at ages 3 and 13 years.

Angelino, Dollins and Mesh (1956), pointed to the role of fears in the education of whole child and concluded that school children, regardless of socio-economic status have about the same number of problems in each of the ten fears and worries categories.

Gesell, Ilg and Ames (1956) indicated that 11 and 12 were the most fearful ages from birth to 16 years age range, with reported fears declining after 12 years of age, though 15 years represented a small peak.

Akutagwa D. (1956) developed first 50 item Fear Survey Schedule. He argued that fears have a dual role: as negative unwanted behavioural tendencies to woke defensive behaviour; and as stimuli to arose repressed fears and anxiety. He also composed a list of fears derived from Jersild and Holmes, study of children; fears taking suggestion from Fenichel's work on Neurosis. This list, he believed provided a broad range of fears common to most people to some degree.

Fear of dark was noted by Lapose and Monk (1959), to decline between the ages of 6 and 12. They also found that girls were more fearful of snakes, strangers, dirt, animals and bugs than boys. Picunas and Clary (1962) found that fear of 'abandonment' by parents increasing between the ages 6 and 12, while 'nightmare' (fears arising during dreams) declining between 6th and 12th year.

Wolpe and Lang (1964) published a 72-item schedule which was derived from FSS 1. This schedule for clinical use. They have described the stimulus situations forming the content of this inventory, as situations to which it would be unadaptive for a person to have anything more than mild anxiety, except perhaps under very special circumstances. The 72 items were classified into six categories, animal (9), social interpersonal (17), tissue damage (18), noises (4), classical phobias (16), Miscellaneous (8)—on the basis of clinical judgement rather than statistical analysis. This schedule is known by the abbreviation, FSS 3.

A further development was published by Gear (1965) on FSS. This schedule was known as FSS 2, comprised 51 items, of which 18 were common to Akutgawa's list, and 20 were common to Wolpe—lang's FSS 3. Gear found significant positive correlations between FSS measures and the Taylor Manifest Anxiety Scale, while with the Social Extraversion/intraversion scale he obtained a very low positive but not significant coefficient.

Maurer (1965) in his study on 82 boys and 30 girls ranging in age from 5½ years to 14½ years, found that boys gave more number of responses than girls, but the difference was not significant. Snakes, lions, tigers and bears predominated the animal category with snakes proving to be most unpopular animal. The things that children were taught to fear (traffic', 'germs', and 'Kidnappers'), were rarely, mentioned. 'Punishment', 'War' and the 'atom-bomb' were also scarce replies.

Manosevity and Lanyon (1965) found out that the mean total fear scores was higher for the females than males. They have put forth two possible explanations that either female actually are more upset and disturbed by the situations assessed in the FSS or females are more honest in reporting their feelings and their fears, possibly because it is more socially undesirable for men than for women to admit to these fears.

Grossberg and Wilson (1965), found that females have significantly higher mean scores that males and also obtained significant positive correlations between FSS measures and the Taylor Manifest Anxiety.

Lanyon and Manosevity (1966) noted that subjects reporting intense' fear of spiders achieved on average scores of 7.29 out of a possible 9.00 on an approach task.

Wolpe and Lazarus (1966) published a schedule which is similar to FSS 3 save for the inclusion of two additional items—looking down from 'high buildings' and 'losing control'—in the former.

Marks and Gelder (1966) studying different ages of onset in varieties of phobia, presented evidence which suggested that fear of animals might, in some way, be different to other fears. It was found that specific animal phobias stood out clearly from the other types of phobia in that most started by the age of 5 years and none started in adult life.

In an experiment Wilson (1967) using a list composed of 18 subject determined 'unreasonable' fears, got 3 male and females 'judges' to rank these fears according to how 'silly' they considered it to be for a person to have an extreme fear of these objects. The fears judged as 'silliest' were reported almost exclusively by females, while the more reasonable fears were reported comparatively more often by males. Wilson concluded that this finding supported a social desirability interpretation of the sex differences frequently observed on the FSS.

Sidna (1967) in his study on 'A comparative study of Fears in Children' found girls to have more fears and no age difference was found in Fear.

Rubin, Katkin and Weiss (1968). Carried out Factorial Analysis on FSS 2. The factors derived for males and females were:

Male	**Female**
Factor 1 – Water Fears	Factor – 1 : Social Competance
Factor 2 – Death & Illness	Factor – 2 : Death Illness
Factor 3 – Interpersonal events	Factor – 3 : Water
Factor 4 – Superstition (Concrete)	Factor – 4 : Social interaction.

The most striking point in the study is the greater degree of homogencity in factor descriptions for females as compared with those for males. Another point of interest is the grouping of fears dealing with death and illness and with performance in the social areas in both the analysis.

A children's schedule (FSS—FC) was published by Scharer & Nakamura (1968). This schedule is intended for children between the ages of 9 and 12 years and the items are categorized into eight areas —School, Home, Social, Physical, Animal, Travel, Classical phobias and Miscellaneous.

Ten factors were extracted from this FSS by Scharer & Nakamura of which five are relatively homogeneous—Fear of Failure, Fear of Criticism, Medical Fears, Fear of Death, Fear of the dark and home/school fears. They also found significant correlations between the children's FSS and children' Manifest Anxiety Scale.

Rubin, Lalis Tastoa, and Namenek (1969), have factor analysed scores obtained in the study from the students using the Lang 122 item FSS. They derived 5 factors which accounted for 90% of the total variance. They were described as Animals, fear of the precipitators, of Hostility, Primitive, Moralistic and sexual fears, fear of isolation or loneliness and fear of anatomical destruction and physical pain.

Agrass *et al* (1969) noted that fears tend to run in families and are especially associated in mothers and daughters. They observed that fears in general have a higher incidence in childhood and tend to fall off during adolescence and early adult life. Only fears of 'death', 'Injury' and 'illness' increase in the order age groups, with the peak in the sixth decade.

Marks (1969) pointed out that the fears of two starting eyes is ubiquitous throughout the animal kingdom including man. He also indicated as Agrass et al that fears in general have a higher incidence in childhood and tend to fall off during adolescence and early adult life.

He also noted that there were hardly any phobias men manifested consistently more than women apart from those concerns specifically with their sexual role.

Lang (1969) developed a 122 item FSS. This schedule was seen as a dual role; as a clinical instrument to assess the kind and relative intensity of the irrational fears of patients, and as a research instrument to measure the relative strength of fear eliciting stimule (This was known as by abbreviation FSS, in literature).

Braun and Reynolds (1969) have published the Temple Fear Survey Inventory which consists of 100 items complied from the published surveys of Gear, Lang and Lazovik, Mansevitz and Lanyon, and Wolpe and Lang.

From the scores obtained in this schedule the investigators made separate analysis of male and female responses, extracting 26 factors from male scores and 28 factors from female scores.

Bernstein and Allen (1969) found female to have significantly higher scores on 17 items out of a total of 51 items. Males had significantly higher mean scores on four items namely 'being in a fight', 'crowded places', 'blood' and 'being with a member of opposite sex'.

Fazio (1969) administered the FSS -III to a group of students of both sexes and assessed their overt approach to an empty glass aquarium containing a cockroach. He found highly significant (P 0.001) negative correlations between subjects proximity to Cockroach and their scores on questionnaire items referring to insects. Similar correlations were not found between proximity and schedule items dealing with *e.g.* worms, speaking in public, people in authority etc.

Spiegler and Libert (1970), explored the self reported fears of 349 volunteers ranging in age from 13 to 85 years. Significant effects for age and sex were obtained. For both sexes, adolescents reported themselves to be significantly more fearful than young adults, where as young adults and adults did not differ in their reported fear for either sex. Senior citizen males, but not females were significantly more fearful than adult males. Adolescents and young adult males reported significantly less fear than their female counter parts. A test of the relationship between the self-reported fear and social desirability on the 145-item questionnaire revealed that the more socially acceptable it was to fear something, the higher the self-reported fear.

Landy and Gaupp (1971) factor analysed the scores they obtained from a student population using FSS III. They extracted 12 factors but only described five, since the remaining seven only accounted for less than 9 per cent of the total variance. The factor described as Factor I: Fear of animate, non-human organisms; Factor II: Interpersonal anxiety; Factor III: fear of the unknown involving magical thinking; Factor IV: noise dimension; Factor V; Fear of medical and surgical procedure.

Wolpe and Lazarus FSS has been factor analyzed by Bates (1971). 17 factors were extracted from the study. He also found significant positive correlations between FSS measures and the Taylor Manifest Anxiety Scale as Hersen (1971).

Lewlis (1971) has factor analysed scores obtained from the study conducted on the students and as well on patients with psychiatric disorders using the Lang (1963) 122 item FSS. He obtained three factors accounting for 90% of the total variance. The factors were fear related to loosing status, fear related to small animals, general fear of disease and wounds. He also obtained significantly higher mean scores for females on 71 items of a 122 item schedule.

Sidana and Sinha (1973) a study on 300 children of 3, 6 and 10 years of age revealed no significant relationship between the fears of 3 year old children and their acceptance by parents, while the middle level rejection of parents at all age levels children had significantly higher mean scores than their counterparts belonging to the low rejection parents group. At the age of 6 children subjected to high independence had less fears.

Rothstein, Holmes and Boblitt (1972) factor analyzed Wolpe and Lazarus (1966) F.S.S. like Bates and they derived 16 factors. Both studies extracted factors loading on tissue damage, social; interpersonal fears (C) noise. The remaining factors in each study bare little relation ships to the other.

Smith's (1974) study on play group children revealed that the social and environmental novelty of a play group to a new child, generally gives rise to some expressions of fear in the short term followed by social and environmental exploration and play. The crowding of a large number of children together in a condition of fixed physical resources cause the elevation of fear responses over a longer term but the responses will be of lower intensity.

Bamber (1974) investigated the self-reported fears and personality characteristics of a sample of 1112 adolescents ranging age between 12-18 years attending Grammar and Secondary schools in Norther Ireland. Analysis of the results indicated that there were considerable sex differences and to a lessor extent difference between intellectual, socio-economic and age groups. Both Grammar and Secondary School girls reported animal fears while boys did not. Grammar and Secondary School boys reported more miscellaneous fears, in which fear of failure was prominent. Secondary school girls had significantly higher F and P scores and neuroticism scores than Grammar girls. On extraversion Grammar school girls scored higher than secondary school girls.

The Wolpe and Lazarus schedule was administered to a sample of 553 girls and 559 boys ranging in age between 12 and 18 years and their responses were factor analysed by Bamber (1977). The most prominent factors to emerge were those loading on items in the social 'stimuli and tissue damage categories. "Tissue damage" items tend to load on a straight "tissue damager" factor a "fear of medical treatment factor" and "fear of unpleasant people" factor, "social stimule" items tend to load on a "social rejection" factor, and on a "fear of exposure in public" factor.

Haste (1978) investigated the attitudes of 3 groups of British undergraduates towards success and failure. The results indicated ambivalence towards success and failure among both sexes. Both indicated some disillusionment with the 'success ethic'. Males showed greater fear about failure.

Darevensky (1979) in his study of children fear found that compared with normal children Educable Mentally Retarded (EMR) Trainable Mentally Retarded (TMR) children exhibited a greater percentage of responses in the categories of animals and a smaller percentage of responses indicating fear of people and natural hazards. For EMR children fear of animals tended to decrease with age. Fear of the dark tended to be the strongest among the TMR children, a larger percentage of these children appeared to fear being alone in the dark, than normal children of the same mental age. In the category nature hazards the answer, received most frequently was "fires" 'death' and 'injury' as a category received a large proportion of responses from all children thus becoming the major fear for most children.

Natarajan's (1979) study on 10th grade students confirmed that fear arousal facilitates the acceptance of the recommend behaviour when it is effective in the immediate reduction of fear arousal. When it is not effective defensive avoidance operates in the higher ranges of fear arousal.

Klopf *et al* (1980) compared the incidence of apprehension about oral communication between 2479 American and 312 Pilpino College students, hypothesizing that there would be no significant difference between the two groups. Result indicated that the pilpinos were significantly less apprehensive than the Americans, thus rejecting the hypothesis.

Singh's *et al* (1980) results of study on 205 upper middle class Indian undergraduates showed that male and females differed both quantitatively and qualitatively on the fear of failure construct. For females significant loadings of fear of failure appeared on two factors—extraversion and age, suggesting that the fear of failure construct is multidimensional.

Singh *et al* (1980) administered a projective test, a culture fair intelligence test, 16 PF test, and the motivation analysis test on 170 undergraduates. Results indicated that 55 with high fear of success scores tended to be intelligent; sensitive; sophisticated; imaginative; interested in arts, home and the opposite sex and regulated by external realities. Significant loadings on fear of success appeared on two factors: fear of success and career orientation. Results supported the conclusion that fear of success is a multidimensional construct.

Khoreshi *et al* (1981) studied 128, 16 to 24 year old subjects, who were paired on age, sex, religion and SES. Analysis showed that Muslims Older SS and upper SES, SS had a greater FOF than their counter parts. There were no such differences on FOF scores.

Vanvaria *et al* (1981) study revealed that Females scored higher on fear of success, tended to be placid, intelligent, anxious about achieving success and some what less interested in sexual satisfaction and comfort. For males there was a close association between fear of success and such variables as warm heartedness 'soberness'. Conscientiousness, relaxation and assertiveness.

Davis *et al* (1981), in their study on the pacing of participant modeling given in 1 long immediate session, delayed 1WK, or divided into 3 weekly sessions was compared when an explanatory rationale was given or withheld with clients exposed to real spiders Vs toy Octopi Imagined as spiders. 91 13-18 yrs. old females secured as Ss. Ss' outcomes were improved by real spiders, by prolonged immediate rather than delayed or spaced sessions, and by rationale provision.

Michel (1981) administered a questionnaire investigating the inventory of fears and worries of 233 female and 573 male Senegalese adolescents. School fears were important in Senegal than in France or the U.S. The number of fears was found to increase with age.

Philip and Garfield (1981) in their study of children's self initiated approach to spiders indicated that males did not show any more approach when paired with females and when not paired they showed more approach. Thus the level of fear interacted with sex of subjects.

Gilroy *et al* (1981) hypothesized that daughters of working mother would demonstrate greater androgyny and less fear of success than the daughters of non-working mothers. Their study on 90 females age 13-17 years supported this hypothesis.

Lohr and Rea (1981) established that fear of public speaking is associated with the personality variable of trait anxiety; trait anxiety was also found to be associated with irrational beliefs. Therapies designed to modify irrational beliefs have been successful in reducing fear about speaking and supported the hypothesis that fear about speech is mediated by irrational beliefs. Their study on 92 undergraduates showed that of only ten beliefs on the Irrational Beliefs Test, demand for approval was positively correlated with scores on the personal report of Public speaking Anxiety.

Duff *et al* (1981) took 20 mildly retarded adults who were matched for CA and sex with non-retarded adults and matched MA and sex with 20 non-retarded children using the P-body picture vocabulary test. SS were given the FSS with a three point rating scale. Retarded subjects were more fearful in general and showed more intense level of fear than their CA matched controls. However they reported less overall fear than the MA matched controls. The importance of understanding the degree and types of fear in promoting deinstitutionalization in the retarded is stressed.

Schwartz *et al* (1981) examined cardiovascular patterns following happiness, sadness, anger, fear, relaxation and control imagery in 32 college students while they were seated and while they exercised. Anger, rather than fear, produced the greatest overall increases in cardiovascular measures and was distinctly opposite from relaxation.

Kartsounis *et al* (1981) investigated the magnitudes and habituation rates of electrodermal orienting responses to phobic or neutral words and phrases that denoted objects or situations feared by the members of a student population. 120 undergraduate subjects reported no fear. The range of potentially phobic stimuli capable of eliciting larger and more slowly habituating ORS (Orienting Responses) was found to be greater than that implied by A. Ohman et al study.

Rigger *et al* (1981) examined the relationship between urban residents fear of crime and fear forms of community involvement. Neighbourhood bonds, residential ties, social interaction with neighbours, and use of local facilities. Data were collected through in person interviews with women living in 3 U.S. cities. Results have shown that while local crime rates were positively correlated with fear, neighbourhood bonds were inversely and more strongly related to fear levels. Residential ties to the community were also related to less fear. However social interaction with neighbours and use of local facilities were not associated with fear levels.

Farley et al (1981) investigated—sex differences and response bias in assessment of fear in 2 studies with 106 female and 106 male undergraduates. The greatest similarity was found between student's normal fears and the patient's fears. Females had significantly greater generalized and extreme fear scores; male simulations most closely reflected this reality.

A compound stimulus, composed of either a fearful, happy or neutral facial expression paired with a neutral cue (tone), signaled an aversive event (mild electric shock). Phasic change in 69 undergraduates skin conductance (SC) was used as the measure of associative learning. Laozetla and Orr's (1981) study on 'stimulus properties of facial expressions and their, influence on the classical conditioning of fear' revealed that Ss who saw a fearful expression paired with tone gave larger SC responses to the fearful expression than to the tone. The opposite pattern was obtained for SS who had a happy expression paired with the tone. SS who had the neutral expression paired with the tone showed no significant differences in their responses to the 2 stimuli. Results support J.T. Lanzetla and S.P. Orr's earlier study and suggest that fear expression function as excitatory stimuli and happy expression act as inhibitory stimuli.

Singh (1981) administered a hostile press measure of fear of failure, along with measures of personality, locus of control, dependence proneness, and neuroticism to 100 female undergraduates. Data support the conclusions that fear of failure is a multidimensional construct, a conception at variance with research. Analysis of behaviour problems suggested that high fear of failure Ss were more anxious, more attention seeking, more depressed and less boisterous and destructive.

Timothy J. *et al* (1981) conducted a study on fourteen year old male. After an intense panic attack at school, became virtually housebound and did not attend school for 5 month prior to therapy, treatment, consisting of self-monitoring, relaxation, thought stopping, imaginal desensitization, and in vivo exposure, ended after 10 weekly sessions when he returned to school. At 18-month follow-up, school records showed nearly perfect attendance and improved grades.

Emil and Fritz (1981) results on inpatient treatment of severe school phobia showed that treatment effectiveness improved if inpatient treatment was followed by suitable aftercare.

Marie, A. and Margaret, R. (1981) described a counseling group conducted with 6 adolescents in an inner city high school. The definition, incidence, and symptomatology of school phobia were included, and the literature on treatment strategies was surveyed. Follow-up data on the participants indicated partial success of the group method.

Kazuhiko and Takeshi (1981) investigated the prevalence of phobic and anxiety symptoms in 1,290 males and 1,210 females (aged

11-23 years). Phobic symptoms were more prevalent in girls except for fear of talking. Among symptoms that tended to appear in anxiety or under stress, frequency of micturition was more prevalent in boys and the remaining symptoms showed not persistent sex difference. Fear of going out of doors alone and feeling of impending death tended to decrease with age. Symptoms that peaked in adolescence (Fear of blushing, fear ofbeing looked at, and most anxiety symptoms) occurred at an earlier age in girls than in boys.

Sartory *et al* (1982) tested the assumption that return of fear could be brought about by recalling highly fear provoking material. Ss were 28 animal—phobia volunteers aged 18-61 years. Two conditions were constrasted in the design, one of which was high Vs. low intensity treatment and the other rehearsal of phobia material Vs. distraction following treatment. It is concluded that rehearsal of fear provoking material following treatment constituted a prolongation of the latter and was therefore therapeutic.

Saigh (1982) developed a norm-referenced Labanese supplement to the FSS to record the incidence and type of war related anxiety reactions. The instrument was administered to 206 Ss (mean age 25-75) years suffering from a wide range of somatic illness. The result revealed that there sex differences among 13 of the items as well as between the total scores.

Shippee *et al* (1982) examined cognitive and affective response of 160 residential dwellers in the aftermath of a flood. Results indicated that respondents who were highly fearful of the disaster were more likely than moderate or low fear respondents to believe that additional flooding would occur in their vacinity and that they resided closer to the flood zone than they actually did.

Punamak (1982) studied attitudes towards war and feelings of fear in 128 Israeli Jewish children, 128 West bank Palestinian Children, and 40 Israeli Arab Children. Palestinian Ss had more traumatic experiences related to war and conflict than did the Israeli Ss. Palestinian Ss showed more fear, and the level of fear was more severe than that of Israelis. Boys in both groups registered less fear than girls. The most severe fears among Palestinian and Israelis Ss related to Ss own and his/her family's security.

Bandura *et al*(1982) in their two experiments combining intergroup and intra-S designs tested the hypothesis that perceived self-efficiency (SE) operates as a cognitive mediator of coping behaviour (CB) and fear arousal (FA). Differential levels of SE were induced in 20 snake and spider—phobic Ss (aged 16-62 years) through inactive mostery or modeling, and their CB and FA were measured. In the next phase, SE was successively raised to designated levels with the same Ss, and their CB and FA were measured again. CB corresponded closely to instated SE, with higher levels of perceived SE being accompanied by greater performance attainments. The SE-action relationship was replicated across different modes of SE and behavioural dysfunctions and in both intergroup and intra-S comparisons.

The hypothesis that FA systems largely from perceived coping inefficacy also received support. Results of Exp. II (12 SS), which used cardiac acceleration and elevation in blood pressure as indicants of FA, further corroborate the generality of the relationship between perceived coping inefficacy and stress reactions.

Anthony and Kevine (1982) in a 3-WK, behaviourally oriented self-control training programme for families, 39 of the 40 participating children (aged 6-13 years) had significantly reduced or completely overcome their severe, chronic nighttime fears. Maintenance of improvement from 2½ to 3½ years without additional treatment and without the occurrence of new problems, was demonstrated in 31 of the 34 follow-up Ss.

Garssen, Veenendaal and Bloemink (1983) investigated the casual relationship between hyperventilation syndrome (HVS) and hyperventilation symptoms (HS). Most patients mentioned the fear of having an attack as an important reason for their agoraphobic complaints.

Ost and Hugdahl (1983) investigated the ways in which the agoraphobic patient acquired their phobia. They concluded that there was no relation between the acquisition and onset of anxiety related to phobic reactions.

Frank *et al* (1982) studied the medical fears of 43 male and 43 female undergraduates using the FSS. The FSS yielded medically relevant fear items.

Klingman *et al* (1982) by administering FSS for children to the border and size of settlement were found to be factors in the fear levels observed. Subjects closer to tension areas had higher fear levels, those from small settlements had higher fear levels than those from medium or large settlements.

To examine the development patterns and genetic influences on common fears Richard and Blaine (1983) studied 10-64 year olds by administering Fear Survey Schedule. Findings suggest significant genetic modulation of developmental patterns in the acquisition and maintenance of some adaptive fears.

Kartsounis L.D. et al (1983) administered an 88-item version of the FSS-III to 547 British undergraduates. Factor analysis revealed 4 main factors, relating to fear of social inadequacy, tissue damage, travel and animals.

Alan D (1983) examined the relationships between 3 & 5 years old children's expressed fears of identifications with animals. The animal named most often as an object of fear was the bear, and the most frequently cited reasons for identification with animals were their perceived strength and abilities to run and jump. Results implied that a fear of being hurt is associated with certain animals, perhaps through stories and the prejudices of adult society.

On a study by Clandette J. and David (1983), on 13-18 yrs/olds indicated that the items that invoked the most fear in males were going to fail, not being promoted in school, impregnating a girl, and being rejected by a member of the opposite sex. For females the items that invoked the most fear one's parent's dying, getting pregnant and failing in school.

John C. and Jack (1983) examined sex differences in the present day fears of 121 3rd grades (71 boys and 50 girls) Results did not support the hypothesis predicting no significant sexual differences in the fears children expressed. Girls wear proportionately more fearful than boys to bugs, snakes, cemeteries, tornadoes, strong winds, strangers, weight, getting and lost and wars. Girls were also more fearful that something bad would happen to their parents.

Klingman *et al* (1983) examined the community intervention procedure of grouping children on the basis of religious attitudes to assess community fear responses. Religious group affiliation was found to be an influential factor in certain fear responses thus supporting the practice of grouping children on the basis of religious attitudes.

Amies, P.L. *et al* (1983) compared 87 16-51 years old social phobics and a 57 20-65 year old agoraphobics to determine whether their respective symptoms were part of distinct syndromes. Results showed that social phobics were younger and more often male, unmarried, and from social classes I and II. Symptoms visible to others were more frequent among social phobics; fainting was of more frequent among the agoraphobics.

William, A *et al* (1983) investigated the degree to which perceived parental attitudes are associated with different subtypes of phobic disorders. Findings revealed that, compared to controls, social and height phobics scored both parents not only as lacking in emotional warmth but also as having been rejective or overprotective. Agoraphobics reported both parents as having lacked emotional warmth but only their mothers as being rejective.

James, F. *et al* (1983) used to desensitization procedure combining the use of emotive imagery play, covert and overt modeling, and behavioural rehearsal in the treatment of 7 year old boy with a severe phobic reaction to dogs. The procedure was effective in eliminating the avoidance behaviour and increasing adaptive social interaction.

Bennett *et al* (1984) investigated two groups of subjects, the characteristics of animals that human are prepared to fear. Fear ratings were significantly correlated with animal characteristics ratings. It was suggested that preparedness to fear certain animals is not a function of the animals per se. but of their fear evoking perceptual properties and their discrepancy from the human form.

In a study conducted by Arlinda A. and James R. (1984); factor analysis of 868 mother's ratings of childrens' fears on the Louisville Fear Survey-Form B yielded oblique primary factors and a higher order general Fearfulness factor at each of 3 age levels between 6 and 16 years. The primary factors were labeled physical Injury, Animals school Related, Night Fears and Fear of Public places. Regression analysis indicated age related decreases in the frequency of fears of Animals Night and Public places, as well as an increase in school—Related fears.

Alan, D. and Colin, R. (1984) administered a questionnaire to 78 undergraduates that included as item asking them to list animals they feared. Results shaved that 87% of Ss who took biology in high school and 77% of Ss who did not list one animal they feared. Appropriate positive experiences with snakes and spiders was suggested for high school biology classes to reduce irrational fears of students.

In a study of Joanne and Glenn G. (1984) 380 parents completed questionnaire on the media content that made their children fearful to investigate the extent to which subject's perceptions would be consistent with predictions based on Piaget's stages of fear developments. It was hypothesized that something that look frightening to a preschool child would elicit fear; while to an order elementary school child, something could happen would be more frightening than something that could not independent of its appearance. Findings suggest that theories of cognitive development could provide an exploratory and predictive frame work for understanding children's fear.

Alan D. (1984) administered a questionnaire to 104 5th graders to survey Ss' fears of animals in the context of gender, experience with pets, and expressed beliefs and affect toward different animal species. Results showed that 73% females and 51% of males reported fears of some animals (snakes, lions, spiders) but pet ownership correlated negatively with fears. It is concluded that contact with animals through pet ownership and care underlies positive feelings about animals and reduces fear of them.

Thomas, H. et al (1985) examined the frequency, intensity and factor structure of fear in 60 males and 66 females (ages 17 to 18 years). Results indicated that females evinced quantitative and qualitative differences from males in the intensity and structure of their self reported fears. The study established the utility of FSSC-R for these age ranges and provided valuable normative data regarding its use.

Thomas, W. and Rebecca, S. (1985) conducted study on longitudinal data on the parent reported fears of 49 pre-school children. The types of fears that were observed were similar to those reported by A. I. Jersild and F. Holmes (1935) nearly 50 years ago. Results indicate that over the last 15 years there had been a substantial increase in preschool childrens fears of the dark, being alone, and strange sights.

Kathleen A (1985) studied 38 female and 62 male 5 and 6 years old children using contextual play technique to gain insight into their fears and worries. Girls appeared to be more concerned about bodily injury both in the contexts of playing at home and at school.

3

Statement of the Problem and Hypotheses

This chapter describes the hypotheses framed, the nature of the sample upon which the study is based and the procedure utilized.

Four separate measures were utilized together data for the present study.

(1) AH_4 Intelligence Test (AH_4).
(2) The Lang's Fear Survey Schedule (FSS).
(3) The Willonghy Neuroticism Schedule (WNS).
(4) The Junior Eysenck Personality Questionnaire (JEPQ).

The following hypotheses have been formulated for the purpose of this investigation.

I. (a) Younger children are likely to have higher fear scores compared to older children.

(b) The younger children will have significantly higher scores on factor of neuroticism compared to older children.

(c) There will be high correlation between the fear scores and neuroticism score.

II. (a) Girls are likely to have significantly higher fear scores than boys.

(b) The Indian adolescents are likely to have more fear scores compared to British adolescents.

III (a) Girls are likely to score high on all the six categories of fear, while boys are likely to score significantly less on categories of miscellaneous, noise and tissue damage fears.

(b) There is likely to be significant difference in the top twelve phobic fears between age groups, gender groups and nationality groups.

Sample

The sample for this study had to consist of both British and Indian adolescents. The sample of British adolescents was drawn from Northern Ireland, U.K. and the Indian sample was drawn from Hyderabad, Andhra Pradesh, India. It comprises a total of 1064 adolescents attending secondary and grammar schools in both the countries.

Indian Sample

A total sample of 524 adolescents was drawn from ten different schools in the twin cities of Hyderabad and Secunderbad in Andhra Pradesh, Southern India.

Eight of the selected schools are Private and Two are managed by the Government. The medium of instruction in the schools selected was English, as these adolescents represent many languages as mother tongue. A sample of 125 girls and 125 boys was drawn from the 12 to 13 years age groups and 140 girls and 134 boys from the 14 to 15 years age groups (Table 3.1).

Education in the state is organised by the education Act (1959-60) the compulsory education is in force. There are five types of schools in the State.

1. Recognised Private Schools (without aid from the Government and run by Private Organisations).
2. Government aided Schools.
3. Government Schools.
4. Andhra Pradesh residential schools, to which admissions are made on a merit basis, employing a test devised by the A.P. Residential Educational Institutional Society.
5. Central Schools.

The government provides free education upto 10th class for boys and Intermediate class for girls. There are a total number of 3,505, 742

Table 3.1 : Indian Sample

S.No.	*Name of the School*	*Type of the School*	*Number of Subjects*	
1.	St. Patrics Boys School	Single Sex	30	Boys
2.	Hyderbad Public School	”	69	”
3.	Govt. Aliya Boys School	”	29	”
4.	Little Flower High School	”	49	”
5.	St. George's Boys School	”	62	”
6.	Central School	Co-education	20	”
	– do –	”	15	Girls
7.	St. Francis High and Secondary Training School	Single Sex	85	”
8.	St. Ann's High School	”	74	”
9.	Govt. Mahabubia Girls Junior College	”	41	”
10.	St. George's Girls Grammar School	”	51	”
		Total :	**525**	

pupils (2,313,066 boys and 1,193,676 girls) attending various educational Institutions in the State.

The percentage of pupils at different stages of education in the twin cities are:

Pre-primary Stage	–	0.2 %
Primary Stage	–	80.0 %
Secondary Stage	–	15.6 %
University Stage	–	1.1 %
Professional and special education for both schools and colleges.	–	3.1%

British Sample

British sample comprising 539 adolescents was drawn from ten different schools of Northern Treland, United Kingdom. The selected schools were equally distributed between grammar and secondary education. Five of the schools were grammar schools and the remaining five schools were secondary schools. The schools selected were also equally distributed between single sex and co-education. Table 3.2 explains the size, type of schools and sex of the adolescents sample drawn.

The total of 539 adolescents were distributed among four sample groups. The size of the each sample group was decided based on the

Table 3.2 : British Sample

S.No.	*Name of the School*	*Type of the School*	*Number of Subjects*	
1.	Royal School, Dungannon	Grammar, Single Sex	60	Boys
2.	St. Michaels Grammar School School, Enniskillen	"	76	"
3.	South Belfast Secondary School, Belfast.	Secondary, Co-education	12	"
	– do –	– do –	19	Girls
4.	Annadale Grammar School, Belfast.	Grammar, Single Sex	48	Boys
5.	Secondary School for Boys, Colerine	Secondary School, Single Sex	32	"
6.	Laurelhill High School, Belfast.	Secondary School, Coeducation	16	"
	-do-	-do-	23	Girls
7.	Wallie Secondary School, Belfast.	Secondary School, Co-education	40	Boys
8.	Girls School, Dungannon	Grammar, Single Sex	54	"
9.	Convent Grammar School, Enniskillen	– do –	30	"
10.	Forthill Secondary School, Belfast.	Secondary, School, Single Sex	41	"
		Total :	539	

factors such as availability of adolescents in the required age and sex groups.

British Sample Group

12 + years Boys	-	125
14 + years Boys	-	159
12 + years girls	-	130
14 + years girls	-	125
Total sample	:	539

The Procedure Utilized

Four separate measures were utilized to gather data for the present study.

I. AH_4 Intelligence Test (AH_4)

AH_4 is a group test to assess general intelligence of the age group of 10 years and over. It is suitable for cross-section of population.

The test comprises of two parts, Part I consisting of 65 questions which have a verbal or numerical bias. Part II consists of 65 questions which have diagrammatic bias and which exemplyfy five types of principle's analogies, sums, substractions, series and superimposition. The assessment of the test is expressed in terms of the total score, that is score on Part I and score on Part II. It is observed that the norms on Part I are somewhat higher than normal on Part II. There is some evidence that this difference is partly due to practice that is to the fact that part II is on the normal course of events, taken immediately after Part I and also to subject is required in Part I, to understand the meaning of every day words and throughout the test, to observe details accurately and to follow simple instructions exactly.

Procedure

Rapport was established between the group of subjects and the tester to enlist the cooperation of subjects. The instructions of the test were given with an introductory remarks. Every subject in the test group was used for the record of time with larger groups of the subjects exceeding 25, the assistance of teachers in the schools was taken while administering the test. Clear instructions were given to the subjects following the manual of AH_4. The time limit for each part was ten minutes, exclusive of the preliminary examples. The time taken for conducting the test was between 30-45 minutes. All the question books and answer sheets were collected from the subjects at the end of testing. One mark is scored for each correct answer. On the form provided on the answer sheet, the subject's marks in Part I, Part II and total scores were entered. The results of the test were treated confidentially.

Consistency

The authors, Heim and Cave (1949) reported a product moment correlation of 0.919 by 100 industrial subjects whose second testing took place one month after their first testing. By reporting on small groups of different intellectual levels they obtained coefficients 0.9. Correlations between scores on part I and scores on part II ranged from 0.81 to 0.60, but for those of highly selected groups of the most intelligent subjects the correlation between the parts varied from 0.70 to 0.83.

Validity

AH_4 has been compared with examination results of school children and university students; with ratings made by University done on their students, by technical college teachers on their pupils and by industrial training officers on their apprentices and trainees. Significant agreement at the 0.05 level has been found between the test and other criteria. For instance a correlation, based on 90 Public school boys, calculated between their AH_4 score on arrival and their term order, at the end of term, yielded an $r = 0.63$.

II. Fear Survey Schedule (FSS)

The purpose of a fear survey schedule in research is to determine both the number and relative strength of fear eliciting stimulus in experimental subjects. The particular form of schedule employed in the present investigation is based on the 122 Item FSS (Leng, 1963). A detailed discussion on development of FSS is given by Bamber (1975).

The following items were omitted from the original schedules.

1. Noise of vacuum cleaner.
2. Being in an elevator.
3. Journeys by airplane.

4. Nude men.
5. Nude women.
6. Being sexually aroused.
7. Homosexual thoughts.
8. Being dressed unsuitable.
9. Being X-rayed.
10. Undertakers.
11. Sexual inadequacy.
12. Masturbation.

The schedule used was modified with the addition of four items.

1. Ghosts.
2. Teachers.
3. Thieves .
4. Unemployment.

These changes were made to match the cultural factors of the subjects.

Certain changes were made for clarity in the wording of original schedule. The changes are as follows:

1. Item 11	-	'Automobiles' to 'Motor cars'.
2. Item 56 & 57	-	'Human blood', 'Animal blood' to 'Blood' (animal or human).
3. Item 69	-	'Premature heart beats' (missing a beat) to 'the heart missing a beat'.
4. Item 79	-	'Becoming nauseous' to 'becoming giddy'.
5. Item 116	-	'Leaving home' to 'Living away from family'.

The questionnaires were given to the subjects selected and asked to fill up. The subjects were asked to pick out those items which they thought, they might find frightening or unpleasant and to enter their schedule number into one of four columns. They were asked to rate their fears for each of 111 items on the inventory on a four point scale. The ratings indicated a 'little' fear was '1', a 'fair amount' '2', much '3' and 'very much' '4'. No column was provided for 'not at all' responses and on tabulation subjects received on '0' for each item which was not communicated in clear way. A copy of the FSS as administered will be found in the appendix-I. Fear Survey schedules have been widely used both for normative data and factor analyses (Bernstein and Allen, 1969, Braun and Reynolds, 1969; Rubin *et al.*, 1968). FSs has been adapted in this investigation as the means of obtaining information about adolescents' fears. An unsatisfactory feature of many studied of fears is the lack of comparability between cultures. In this study Fear Survey Schedule is utilized to find out and interpret the total fear scores achieved and the intensity of fear.

III. Willoughby Neuroticism Schedule (WNS)

The willoughby Neuroticism schedule has been extensively used as a test of neuroticism. The persistent unadaptive anxiety reactions and the neuroticism revealed by the questionnaire relates mainly to common types of social situations. This schedule is an abridged version of Clerk-thurston Inventory (Willoughy, 1932) which consisted of 25 items. According to willoughby the neurotic personality is characterised by inner fears and anxieties and corresponding inability to establish effective contact with the social environment.

Willoughby Neuroticism schedule was used by Wolpe in behaviour therapy and he regards a score of 15-20 on the schedule as indicating the border line between normality and neurotic personality.

Bamber (1974) in his study of a 1112 adolescent population found that 'Neuroticism' measured by WNS was not identical to the 'Neuroticism' measured by Eysenck personality Inventory. He attributes this difference to the universal nature of neuroticism in WNS. The Willoughby Neuroticism schedule is utilized in the present study because of its use in previous studies of fears. The schedule is enclosed in appendix-II.

IV. Junior Eysenck Personality Questionnaire (JEPQ)

Eysenck personality questionnaire (Junior 1975, EPQ) is the improvised scale of PEN Inventory (Eysenck, 1969) for children. It measures the three factors, extraversions (E) neurocism (N) and psychoticism (P). It is a development of various earlier personality questionnaires. It is used for normal children with age range 7 to 15 years. The final version of EPQ (Junior) consists of 81 items breaking down into four major factors namely, E (24), N (20), P(17) and L(20). The new scale differs from the other by including an additional scale the P scale and having certain improvements made to the other scales.

The child with high p score is described as an odd, isolated, troublesome, glacial and lacking in human feelings for his fellow-beings and for animals. They are aggressive and hostile even to near and dear ones. The typical extrovert is described as sociable, likes parties, has many friends, needs to have people to talk to and does not like reading or studying by himself. An introvert is a quiet, retiring sort of person, introspective, fond of books rather than people, he is reserved and distant except to intimate friends.

The scale was found to be highly reliable (0.74) and the internal consistency of the scale was quite independent of the degrees of motivation for dissimulation.

One month test retest data for older children (12 to 14 years) range from an extremely low figure of 0.55 to 0.89. The reliabilities of the E, N and L scales are all with the 0.7 to 0.9 and those for P are a little below the 0.7 value. Reliabilities are rather low for the younger children in Test-Retest reliabilities with 6 months intervening between testings. From the age of 10 years onwards, reliabilities are above 0.6 (Eysenck S.B.G., and Eysenck, H.T.L., 1975).

Instructions for completion of the J.E.P.Q. are printed on each copy (Appendix-III). When the questionnaires were collected from the subjects after completion, care was taken to check that all questions had been answered. The questionnaires were scored by using the appropriate scoring sheets.

Though JEPQ was not standardized in India it was considered safe to use it, since the results of a study by Verma S.K. and Cvig N.N. (1972) using an earlier version of the questionnaire, the PEN Inventory suggested little influence of cultural differences. In another study by Prasad *et al*, 1974, which also used the PEN Inventory in addition to various other questionnaires, a statistical analysis resulted in three clusters, which were identified by the investigator as Neuroticism, Extroversion and Psychoticism.

The following statistical techniques were utilized for analysis of data.

(1) Fisher's '+' Test

Differences of age, gender and type of nationality were compared by applying a '+' tests.

(2) Pearson Product Moment Correlations

Pearson Product Moment correlation and co-efficients were calculated to find out the relationship between phobic and fear scores and Willoughby Neuroticism scores, ('P' and 'F' scores and Willoughby 'Neuroticism scores) and WNS Total score and JEPQ Scores.

(3) Analysis of Variance

Analysis of variance is carried out to find out the age, gender and type of nationality difference in phobic fears of all the sample groups.

4
Methods and Procedure

This chapter presents the results of the study consisting of Part–I and Part–II. Part–I has three sections, containing findings of age, gender and nationality differences among the sample groups compared.

Part–II consists of two section describing the variations on the mean scores of fear items on FSS and phobic fears of adolescents compared for age, gender and nationality differences.

PART—I

Section—1

The Findings on Age Differences

The results of all tests administered to the Indian and British sample were compared between 12 yrs. and 14 yrs. aged groups. They are presented in this chapter under the following headings.

1. AH_4 Intelligence (AH_4).
2. P and F scores on Fear Survey Schedule (FSS).
3. Willoughby Neurotism Schedule (WNS).
4. Junior Eysenck Personality Questionnaire (JEPQ).
5. Correlation comparisons by age.

Table 4.4, 4.5 and 4.6 shows the significance of differences of means by age for all the sample groups using Fisher's 'T' test. The correlations between all the tests by sample groups were described in Tables.

Differences in Intelligence

AH_4 Intellingence Test

Significant age differences were found between the scores on the intelligence tests. Three sample group of 14 years old compared with 12 years old displayed an increase in scores on intelligence with the difference reaching beyond the 1% level of significance. The score of Indian girls of 14 years of age were not significantly different from the 12 years age group of Indian girls on mean scores for the verbal part of the intelligence test. However, they had shown significant differences at the level of0.01 (Table 4.1) both on non-verbal and total scores of AH_4 test. The mean scores of all 14 years age groups on AH_4 (total) scores were significantly higher than the 12 years age group, indicating an increase of total scores with age.

Table 4.1 : Significance of the Differences between Means by Sample Groups Aged 12 Years and 14 Years Adolescents on AH_4 Intelligence Test

Sample Groups Compared	*Verbal*		*Non-verbal*		*Total*	
	Mean	*CR*	*Mean*	*CR*	*Mean*	*CR*
Indian Boys 12 yrs.	31.98		38.35		70.25	
Vs.		5.58***		4.60***		5.74***
Indian Boys 14 yrs.	38.52		44.55		83.07	
Indian Girls 12 yrs.	28.02		31.48		59.14	
Vs.		1.77		3.07**		2.89**
Indian Girls 14 yrs.	30.12		35.80		65.99	
British Boys 12 yrs.	41.18		48.58		89.84	
Vs.		6.52***		6.24***		7.13***
British Boys 14 yrs.	48.07		55.56		103.62	
British Girls 12 yrs.	38.45		43.49		81.94	
Vs.		8.75***		6.83***		8.31***
British Girls 14 yrs.	49.33		42.46		101.74	

* – 0.05 ** – 0.01 *** – 0.001

Comparison of Phobias and Fears

'P' and 'F' Scores on FSS

The comparison of age difference was confined to the 'P' (Phobic) and 'F' (Total fear score) scores on the FSS.

The mean 'P' score of a sample group is the mean of the sum of entries in column 4 under 'very much' on FSS for each sample member. The mean 'F' score for a sample is the mean of the sum of all items registered on the schedule for each sample member.

With the exception of Indian boys there are not significant difference between the means of 'P' and 'F' scores on FSS (Table 4.2). Significant differences were noted between the means for 12 years and 14 years Indian boys on P and F fear scores. 14 years old Indian boys scored significantly higher P and F scores than 12 years old Indian boys.

Table 4.2 : Significance of the Differences between Means by Sample Groups Aged 12 Years and 14 Years Adolescents on Fear Survey Schedule

Sample Groups Compared	*FSS 'P' Score*		*FSS 'F' Score*	
	Mean	*CR*	*Mean*	*CR*
Indian Boys 12 yrs.	10.99		120.14	
Vs.		2.92**		2.18*
Indian Boys 14 yrs.	14.53		138.39	
Indian Girls 12 yrs.	17.14		149.12	
Vs.		0.65		0.15
Indian Girls 14 yrs.	18.09		159.53	
British Boys 12 yrs.	8.28		85.55	
Vs.		7.26		0.01
British Boys 14 yrs.	6.80		85.65	
British Girls 12 yrs.	15.35		131.11	
Vs.		0.48		1.08
British Girls 14 yrs.	14.57		140.50	

* – 0.05   ** – 0.01   *** – 0.001

Differences an Neurotism

Willoughby Neurotism Schedule Scores

British boys revealed no significant age differences on any of the WNS scores. Indian boys of 12 years had significantly higher mean scores for Liability of mood (IV factor on WNS) compared with 14 years age group. Indian girls showed a reversed picture on the same factor. Indian girls of 12 years age group had significantly lower mean scores on Liability of mood compared with 14 years old girls.

An interesting finding with age differences was the higher mean scores of the 14 years age group girls on the total WNS score. 14 years old Indian girls reached the level of significance on the fear of self-exposure, Liability of mood and Lack of self-confidence factors. British girls of 14 years age significantly differed from 12 years girls on Hypertensitivity, and lack of self-confidence factors. (Table 4.3).

Personality Differences

Junior Eysench Personality Questionnaire (JEPQ)

Significant differences were found on Extraversion in the Indian sample groups. Indian boys of 14 years had a significantly higher mean score than 12 years old Indian boys on Extraversion. But Indian girls indicated the opposite results showing a significantly lower mean score with age on Extraversion. Indian girls aged 12 years had a significantly higher mean score than Indian girls aged 14years on Extraversion (Table 4.4).

Significant differences were noted on Extraversion for Indian boys and girls of 14 years old. However, the level of significance failed to reach 0.01 level for girls.

There were no significant age differences on the dimension of Neurotism. Both British and Indian girls of 14 years revealed difference on Psychotism at 0.05 level of significance. British girls indicated a significance difference on Lie score. It declined with age.

Correlational Comparisons

Correlational comparisons denote the relationship between various factors in all the tests conducted. Correlation co-efficient between P score and 5 factors and total score of WNS. (Factor I—General neurotic factor, Factor II—Fear of self exposure, Factor III—uncertainty

Table 4.3 : Significance of the Differences between Means for Sample Groups Aged 12 years and 14 years Adolescents on Willoughby Neuroticism Schedule (WNS)

Sample Groups Compared	WS FI		WNS FII		WNS FIII		WNS FIV		WNS FV		WNS Total	
	Mean	CR	Mean	CR	Mean	CR	Mean	CR	Mean	CR	Mean	CR
Indian Boys 12 yrs.	6.30		4.24		7.09		5.01		8.27		30.56	
Vs.		0.47		0.07		0.97		2.07*		0.47		0.27
Indian Boys 14 yrs.	6.05		4.26		6.55		4.58		6.99		28.38	
Indian Girls 12 yrs.	5.57		2.94		6.27		3.57		6.09		24.43	
Vs.		1.041		3.22**		1.95		2.21		2.30*		3.87***
Indian Girls 14 yrs.	6.12		4.01		7.21		4.65		7.44		29.44	
British Boys 12 yrs.	6.08		6.08		7.26		6.76		10.03		36.6	
Vs.		1.05		1.09		1.41		0.65		1.24		0.36
British Boys 14 yrs.	6.59		5.67		7.98		7.04		9.31		35.99	
British Girls 12 yrs.	1.56		6.08		7.48		7.88		9.83		38.53	
Vs.		2.76**		0.96		0.80		1.16		2.02*		1.96*
British Girls 14 yrs.	9.10		5.67		7.90		8.46		11.14		42.50	

* – 0.05 ** – 0.01 *** – 0.001

Table 4.4 : Significance of the Differences between Means for Sample Groups Aged 12 years and 14 years Adolescents on JEPQ

Sample Groups Compared	*JEPQ*		*JEPQ*		*JEPQ*		*JEPQ*	
	Mean	*CR*	*Mean*	*CR*	*Mean*	*CR*	*Mean*	*CR*
Indian Boys 12 yrs.	15.38		8.68		5.01		11.66	
Vs.		3.05**		0.18		1.06		1.44
Indian Boys 14 yrs.	16.99		8.60		4.65		12.16	
Indian Girls 12 yrs.	15.95		8.19		3.84		14.55	
Vs.		2.16*		0.03		2.91**		1.01
Indian Girls 14 yrs.	15.24		8.18		4.76		13.13	
British Boys 12 yrs.	18.78		12.16		4.99		4.79	
Vs.		0.21		1.46		1.34		0.53
British Boys 14 yrs.	18.88		11.47		4.53		4.99	
British Girls 12 yrs.	18.72		18.72		2.39		7.48	
Vs.		1.61		1.61		2.15*		3.89**
British Girls 14 yrs.	17.88		17.88		3.00		5.61	

* – 0.05 ** – 0.01 *** – 0.001

and social timidity, Factor IV—Lability of made, Factor V—Lack of self-confidence and social inadequacy) and P score with Extraversion, neurotism, Psychotisum and Lie score factors of JEPQ were presented. In similar way correlations between F scores and factors of WNS and JEPQ were described. Lastly correlations between WNS total score and ENPL factors of JEPQ were given in (Table 4.5).

(a) Correlations between P Score and WNS

There was difference of age between P scores and WNS factors for Indian boys. There were no significant correlation coefficients obtained between P score and WNS factors for 12 years boys and significant positive coefficient values were obtained between P score and general factors neurotic factor, uncertainty and social timidity and total score of WNS for 14 years old boys. The trend was different for Indian girls. They showed significant positive correlation coefficients between P score and all WNS factors with an exception of 14 years old girls on the third factor of WNS. 14 years Indian girls did not show significant correlation between P score and uncertainity and social timidity of WNS and moderate correlations in all other factors.

British boys of both the age groups revealed significant positive correlations between P score and WNS factors general neurotic factor fear of self-exposure and total score. The remaining factors did not indicate significant values. British girls showed uniform significant positive correlations between P score and WNS factors except in fear of self-exposure. 14 years British girls did not have significant correlations between fear of self-exposure and P score, while 12 years old British girls showed significant positive correlation at 0.01 level. [Tables 4.7(a)].

There is no significant correlations between P score and factors of JEPQ for both the age groups of Indian boys and girls with an exception of 14 years girls. There are significant positive correlations between P score and extraversion of JEPQ at 0.05 level for 14 years Indian girls. British boys and girls obtained positive low significant coefficients between P score and neuroticism of JEPQ.

(b) Correlations between F Scores and WNS and JEPQ

The correlations coefficients obtained between F score and Willoughby Neurotic Schedule factors were positively and significant for the 12 years and 14 years age groups of Indian boys, within all the factors with the exception of one factor *i.e.*, Lability of Mood. The value of correlation coefficient between F score and Lability of Mood is not significant for 12 years Indian boys. Indian boys of 14 years had more high and significant correlation coefficients than 12 years groups.

The Indian girls of both the age groups and significant positive coefficient between F score and all the factors of WNS.

Significant positive correlations were noted between F score and all the factors of WNS for British boys. But 12 years British boys did not show any significant correlations between F scores and fear of Self-Exposure and Lability of Mood where as 14 years boys group revealed no significant correlation between F score and lack of self-confidence and 'Social Inadequacy'.

Indian boys of both the age groups revealed significant correlations between F score and Psychotism and negative significant correlation between F scores and Lie score of JEPQ. There were significant correlations between F scores and factors of JEPQ for Indian girls. There was no significant correlation between F score and extraversion for both the age groups of British boys. Positive significant correlations were found between F score and neurotism and Lie score for 12 years British boys. The significant correlation observed between F score and neurotism for 14 years British boys was negative.

(c) Correlation between Scores of WNS and JEPQ

There was significant positive correlation between WNS and neurotism, psychotism and Lie Negative correlation were found between WNS and Extraversion for Indian boys of both the age groups. Indian girls had significant positive correlations between WNS and Extraversion and Neurotism factors.

British 14 years boys indicated negative correlations between WNS and Extraversion, L scores and Positive correlation between WNS and N scores, While 12 years boys had positive correlations between WNS and Neurotism scores. British girls of both the age groups denoted positive correlation between WNS and E and N factors of JEPQ.

Table 4.5 : PEARSON PRODUCT MOMENT CORRELATIONS FOR 12 YEARS AND 14 YEARS OLD INDIAN GIRLS SAMPLE GROUPS AND ALL THE TESTS

Table 4.5(a) : Correlations between 'P' Score and Factors of WNS

Tests Correlated	*Indian Girls*	
	12 years	*14 years*
FSS 'P' Score *Vs.* WNS Factor I	0.318**	0.180*
FSS 'P' Score *Vs.* WNS Factor II	0.235**	0.200*
FSS 'P' Score *Vs.* WNS Factor III	0.348**	0.121*
FSS 'P' Score *Vs.* WNS Factor IV	0.320**	0.195*
FSS 'P' Score *Vs.* WNS Factor V	0.303**	0.168*
FSS 'P' Score *Vs.* WNS Total Score	0.428**	0.224*

* – 0.05 ** – 0.01

Table 4.5(b) : Correlations between 'P' Score and Factors of JEPQ

Tests Correlated	*Indian Girls*	
	12 years	*14 years*
FSS 'P' Score *Vs.* EPQ 'E' Score	0.123	0.170*
FSS 'P' Score *Vs.* EPQ 'N' Score	0.153	0.034
FSS 'P' Score *Vs.* EPQ 'P' Score	0.080	0.045
FSS 'P' Score *Vs.* EPQ 'L' Score	0.060	0.036

* – 0.05 ** – 0.01

Table 4.5(c) : Correlations between 'F' Score and Factors of WNS

Tests Correlated	*Indian Girls*	
	12 years	*14 years*
FSS 'F' Score *Vs.* WNS Factor I	0.284**	0.296**
FSS 'F' Score *Vs.* WNS Factor II	0.251**	0.266
FSS 'F' Score *Vs.* WNS Factor III	0.314**	0.240**
FSS 'F' Score *Vs.* WNS Factor IV	0.290	0.230
FSS 'F' Score *Vs.* WNS Factor V	0.304**	0.248**
FSS 'F' Score *Vs.* WNS Total Score	0.407**	0.335**

* – 0.05 ** – 0.01

Table 4.5(d) : Correlations between 'F' Score and Factors of JEPQ

Tests Correlated	*Indian Girls*	
	12 years	*14 years*
FSS 'F' Score *Vs.* EPQ 'E' Score	0.179*	0.010
FSS 'F' Score *Vs.* EPQ 'N' Score	0.120	0.027
FSS 'F' Score *Vs.* EPQ 'P' Score	0.010	0.004
FSS 'F' Score *Vs.* EPQ 'L' Score	0.051	0.110

* – 0.05

Table 4.5(e) : Correlations between WNS Total and Factor of JEPQ

Tests Correlated	*Indian Girls*	
	12 years	*14 years*
WNS Total *Vs.* EPQ 'E'	0.188*	0.238**
WNS Total *Vs.* EPQ 'N'	0.324**	0.292**
WNS Total *Vs.* EPQ 'P'	0.075	0.059
WNS Total *Vs.* EPQ 'L'	0.136	–0.079

* – 0.05 ** – 0.01

Table 4.6 : PEARSON PRODUCT MOMENT CORRELATIONS FOR 12 YEARS AND 14 YEARS INDIAN BOYS ON ALL THE TESTS

Table 4.6(a) : Correlations between 'P' Score and Factors of WNS

Tests Correlated	*Indian Boys*	
	12 years	*14 years*
FSS 'P' Score *Vs.* WNS Factor I	0.124	0.213*
FSS 'P' Score *Vs.* WNS Factor II	0.061	0.062
FSS 'P' Score *Vs.* WNS Factor III	0.095	0.340**
FSS 'P' Score *Vs.* WNS Factor IV	0.004	0.136
FSS 'P' Score *Vs.* WNS Factor V	0.078	0.171
FSS 'P' Score *Vs.* WNS Total Score	0.090	0.256**

* – 0.05 ** – 0.01

Table 4.6(b) : Correlations between 'P' Score and Factors of JEPQ

Tests Correlated	*Indian Boys*	
	12 years	*14 years*
FSS 'P' Score *Vs.* EPQ 'E' Score	0.053	0.137
FSS 'P' Score *Vs.* EPQ 'N' Score	0.032	0.013
FSS 'P' Score *Vs.* EPQ 'P' Score		0.056
FSS 'P' Score *Vs.* EPQ 'L' Score	0.012	0.059

Table 4.6(c) : Correlations between 'F' Score and Factors of WNS

Tests Correlated	*Indian Boys*	
	12 years	*14 years*
FSS 'F' Score *Vs.* WNS Factor I	0.176*	0.311**
FSS 'F' Score *Vs.* WNS Factor II	0.200*	0.238**
FSS 'F' Score *Vs.* WNS Factor III	0.221*	0.410**
FSS 'F' Score *Vs.* WNS Factor IV	0.109	0.294**
FSS 'F' Score *Vs.* WNS Factor V	0.230**	0.302**
FSS 'F' Score *Vs.* WNS Total Score	0.243**	0.414**

* – 0.05 ** – 0.01

Table 4.6(d) : Correlations between 'F' Score and Factors of JEPQ

Tests Correlated	*Indian Boys*	
	12 years	*14 years*
FSS 'F' Score *Vs.* EPQ 'E' Score	0.092	0.151
FSS 'F' Score *Vs.* EPQ 'N' Score	0.151	0.031
FSS 'F' Score *Vs.* EPQ 'P' Score	0.191*	0.233**
FSS 'F' Score *Vs.* EPQ 'L' Score	(–)0.205*	(–)0.101*

* – 0.05 ** – 0.01

Table 4.6(e) : Correlations between WNS Total and Factor of JEPQ

Tests Correlated	*Indian Boys*	
	12 years	*14 years*
WNS Total *Vs.* EPQ 'E'	(–) 0.228**	(–)0.338**
WNS Total *Vs.* EPQ 'N'	0.436**	0.272**
WNS Total *Vs.* EPQ 'P'	0.296**	0.359**
WNS Total *Vs.* EPQ 'L'	(–)0.375**	(–)0.230**

* – 0.05 ** – 0.01

Table 4.7 : PEARSON PRODUCT MOMENT CORRELATIONS FOR 12 YEARS BRITISH GIRLS ON ALL THE TESTS

Table 4.7(a) : Correlations between 'P' Score and Factors of WNS

Tests Correlated	*British Girls*	
	12 years	*14 years*
FSS 'P' Score *Vs.* WNS Factor I	0.260**	0.389**
FSS 'P' Score *Vs.* WNS Factor II	0.272**	0.093
FSS 'P' Score *Vs.* WNS Factor III	0.225*	0.435**
FSS 'P' Score *Vs.* WNS Factor IV	0.221*	0.172
FSS 'P' Score *Vs.* WNS Factor V	0.314*	0.292**
FSS 'P' Score *Vs.* WNS Total Score	0.328**	0.367**

* – 0.05 ** – 0.01

Table 4.7(b) : Correlations between 'P' Score and Factors of JEPQ

Tests Correlated	*British Girls*	
	12 years	*14 years*
FSS 'P' Score *Vs.* EPQ 'E' Score	0.049	0.018
FSS 'P' Score *Vs.* EPQ 'N' Score	0.191	0.313**
FSS 'P' Score *Vs.* EPQ 'P' Score	0.011	0.048
FSS 'P' Score *Vs.* EPQ 'L' Score	0.170	0.024

** – 0.01

Table 4.7(c) : Correlations between 'F' Score and Factors of WNS

Tests Correlated	*British Girls*	
	12 years	*14 years*
FSS 'F' Score *Vs.* WNS Factor I	0.331**	0.414**
FSS 'F' Score *Vs.* WNS Factor II	0.321**	0.155
FSS 'F' Score *Vs.* WNS Factor III	0.292**	0.438**
FSS 'F' Score *Vs.* WNS Factor IV	0.192*	0.211*
FSS 'F' Score *Vs.* WNS Factor V	0.305**	0.334**
FSS 'F' Score *Vs.* WNS Total Score	0.368**	0.416**

* – 0.05 ** – 0.01

Table 4.7(d) : Correlations between 'F' Score and Factors of WNS

Tests Correlated	*British Girls*	
	12 years	*14 years*
FSS 'F' Score *Vs.* EPQ 'E' Score	(–)0.204*	0.014
FSS 'F' Score *Vs.* EPQ 'N' Score	0.248**	0.356**
FSS 'F' Score *Vs.* EPQ 'P' Score	0.061	0.039
FSS 'F' Score *Vs.* EPQ 'L' Score	0.244**	0.002

* – 0.05 ** – 0.01

Table 4.7(e) : Correlations between WNS Total and Factors of JEPQ

Tests Correlated	*British Girls*	
	12 years	*14 years*
WNS Total *Vs.* EPQ 'E'	0.346**	0.204*
WNS Total *Vs.* EPQ 'N'	0.451**	0.573**
WS Total *Vs.* EPQ 'P'	0.025	0.080
WNS Total *Vs.* EPQ 'L'	0.062	0.055

* – 0.05 ** – 0.01

Table 4.8 : PEARSON PRODUCT MOMENT CORRELATIONS FOR 12 YEARS AND 14 YEARS BRITISH BOYS ON ALL THE TESTS

Table 4.8(a) : Correlations between 'P' Score and Factors of WNS

Tests Correlated	*British Boys*	
	12 years	*14 years*
FSS 'P' Score *Vs.* WNS Factor I	0.180*	0.272**
FSS 'P' Score *Vs.* WNS Factor II	0.037	0.117
FSS 'P' Score *Vs.* WNS Factor III	0.071	0.119
FSS 'P' Score *Vs.* WNS Factor IV	0.028	0.110
FSS 'P' Score *Vs.* WNS Factor V	0.286**	0.158*
FSS 'P' Score *Vs.* WNS Total Score	0.192*	0.201*

* – 0.05 ** – 0.01

Table 4.8(b) : Correlations between 'P' Score and Factors of JEPQ

Tests Correlated	*British Boys*	
	12 years	*14 years*
FSS 'P' Score *Vs.* EPQ 'E' Score	0.090	0.040
FSS 'P' Score *Vs.* EPQ 'N' Score	0.192	0.176*
FSS 'P' Score *Vs.* EPQ 'P' Score	0.45	0.059
FSS 'P' Score *Vs.* EPQ 'L' Score	0.210	0.088

* – 0.05

Table 4.8(c) : Correlations between 'P' Score and Factors of WNS

Tests Correlated	*British Boys*	
	12 years	*14 years*
FSS 'F' Score *Vs.* WNS Factor I	0.308**	0.348**
FSS 'F' Score *Vs.* WNS Factor II	0.135	0.207*
FSS 'F' Score *Vs.* WNS Factor III	0.193*	0.175*
FSS 'F' Score *Vs.* WNS Factor IV	0.109	0.169*
FSS 'F' Score *Vs.* WNS Factor V	0.312**	0.158
FSS 'F' Score *Vs.* WNS Total Score	0.304**	0.261**

* – 0.05 ** – 0.01

Table 4.8(d) : Correlations between 'F' Score and Factors of JEPQ

Tests Correlated	*British Boys*	
	12 years	*14 years*
FSS 'F' Score *Vs.* EPQ 'E' Score	0.080	0.002
FSS 'F' Score *Vs.* EPQ 'N' Score	0.288**	–0.238**
FSS 'F' Score *Vs.* EPQ 'P' Score	0.028	0.022
FSS 'F' Score *Vs.* EPQ 'L' Score	0.178*	0.002

* – 0.05 ** – 0.01

Table 4.8(e) : Correlations between WNS Total and Factors of JEPQ

Tests Correlated	*British Boys*	
	12 years	*14 years*
WNS Total *Vs.* EPQ 'E'	0.096	0.294**
WNS Total *Vs.* EPQ 'N'	0.514**	0.528**
WNS Total *Vs.* EPQ 'P'	0.010	0.059
WNS Total *Vs.* EPQ 'L'	0.014	–0.232**

* – 0.05 ** – 0.01

Section — 2

In this section findings on the gender differences are presented by comparing boys sample groups with girls sample groups. The results are given as follows:

(1) Comparisons on AH_4 Intelligence scores.
(2) P and F score of FSS.
(3) Willoughbhy neuroticism schedule.
(4) Junior Eysenck Personality Questionnaire.
(5) Correlational comparison by boy-girl differences.

THE FINDINGS ON GENNDER DIFFERENCES

Differences in Intelligence

AH_4 Intelligence Test

Boys differ from girls showing significantly higher mean scores than girls in AH_4 Intelligence test. The gender differences were significantly marked in all parts of AH_4 test except in case of 14 years old British boys and girls. The differences were not significant between boys and girls of this sample groups in AH_4 verbal and AH_4 total scores of the test. The only part of the test in which significant gender differences were found was AH_4 non-verbal indicating higher mean scores of boys in all sample groups.

The gender differences were clearly marked in Intelligence test in favour of boys (Table 4.9).

Table 4.9 : Significance of the Differences between Means by Sample Groups with Age Constant on AH_4 Intelligence Test

Sample Groups Compared	*Verbal*		*Non-verbal*		*Total*	
	Mean	*CR*	*Mean*	*CR*	*Mean*	*CR*
Indian Boys 12+ yrs.	31.98		38.35		70.25	
Vs.		3.295***		4.67***		
Indian Girls 12+ yrs.	28.02		31.48		49.14	
Indian Boys 14+ yrs.	38.52		44.55		83.08	
Vs.		7.23***		6.74***		
Indian Girls 14+ yrs.	30.12		35.80		65.99	
British Boys 12+ yrs.	41.18		48.58		89.84	
Vs.		2.31*		3.77***		3.40
British Girls 12+ yrs.	38.45		43.49		81.94	
British Boys 14+ yrs.	48.07		55.56		103.62	
Vs.		1.12		2.88**		0.94
British Girls 14+ yrs.	49.33		52.46		101.74	

* – 0.05 ** – 0.01 *** – 0.001

Comparison of Phobias on Fears

'P' and 'F' Scores on FSS

Boys sample groups of both nationalities significantly differed from girls sample groups with low means of P and F scores on FSS.

However this difference was marked at 0.01 significance level for 14 yrs. Indian boys and girls ant at 0.001 level for other sample groups. Girls sample groups were clearly differentiated from boys sample groups with significantly higher P and F scores on FSS. (Table 4.10).

Table 4.10 : Significance of the Differences between Means by Sample Groups on FSS

Sample Groups Compared	*FSS 'P' Score*		*FSS 'F' Score*	
	Mean	*CR*	*Mean*	*CR*
Indian Boys 12+ yrs.	10.99		120.14	
Vs.		4.66***		3.51***
Indian Girls 12+ yrs.	17.14		149.12	
Indian Boys 14+ yrs.	14.53		138.39	
Vs.		2.61**		2.46**
Indian Girls 14+ yrs.	19.08		159.53	
British Boys 12+ yrs.	8.24		85.55	
Vs.		4.92***		5.82***
British Girls 12+ yrs.	15.35		53.38	
British Boys 14+ yrs.	6.81		85.65	
Vs.		5.99***		7.62***
British Girls 14+ yrs.	14.57		140.50	

* – 0.05 ** – 0.01 *** – 0.001

Differences in Neuroticism

Willoughby Neurotism Schedule (WNS)

Indian boys of 12 years age groups had higher mean scores and significant differences compared with the girls on Fear of Self exposure (II Factor), Lability of Mood (IV Factor), Lack of Self-confidence and Social Inadequacy (V Factor) and total score of the test. They did not differ from girls significantly on general neurotic factor (I Factor) and uncertainity and Social timidity (III Factor). The opposite trend was observed with British sample groups. Girls had higher mean scores on all the significance differences. The only sample group which did not have any significant gender differences on this schedule was 14 years Indian boys and girls. The only part of WNS on which no significant differences was noted was the III factor of Uncertainity and Social Timidity. Only British sample groups had significant gender differences on general neurotic factor of WNS with higher mean scores for girls (Table 4.11).

Personality Differences

Junior Eysenck Personality Questionnaire (JEPQ)

The gender differences were clearly marked on the scores of this questionnaire. Girls in all the sample groups significantly differed from boys exhibiting higher mean scores on Lie scale. Boys and higher mean scores on extraversion and Psychotism in all the significant differences, while girls had higher mean scores on Neurotism. Both Indian and British sample groups of 12 years age did not have any significant differences on Extraversion. Indian boys and girls of both the age groups did not differ significantly on Neurotism and Psychotism factors of the questionnaire. British sample of 14 years age group showed significant gender differences on all the factors of JEPQ, with higher mean scores of girls on Neurotism and Lie scale, and boys with higher mean scores on Extraversion and Psychotism (Table 4.12).

Correlation Comparisons

1. Gender Differences

(a) Correlations between P Score and WNS and P Score and JEPQ

Indian Girls of 12 years age group differ from boys of the same age group boys showing significant positive correlations with all WNS factors. Boys of the same age group show the reverse picture by indicating no significant correlations between 'P' Score and WNS factors.

There is no clear boy-girl differences between 'P' Scores and WNS among 14 years Indian group. Both boys and girls groups show positive significant correlations. However the number of significant correlations indicated are more for girls than boys.

Table 4.11 : Significance of the Differences between Means by Sample Groups with Age Constant on WNS Gender Differences

Sample Groups Compared	*WNS FI*		*WNS FII*		*WNS FSII*		*WNS FIV*		*WNS FV*		*WNS Total*	
	Mean	*CR*	*Mean*	*CR*	*Mean*	*CR*	*Mean*	*CR*	*Mean*	*CR*	*Mean*	*CR*
Indian Boys 12+ yrs.	6.30		7.09		7.09		5.01		8.27		30.56	
Vs.				5.29**		1.52		2.86**		3.56**		3.17**
Indian Girls 12+ yrs.	5.57		2.93		6.27		3.57		6.09		24.43	
Indian Boys 14+ yrs.	6.05		4.26		4.58		4.58		6.99		28.38	
Vs.		0.14		0.71		1.47		0.16		0.68		0.57
Indian Girls 14+ yrs.	6.12		4.01		7.21		4.65		7.44		29.44	
British Boys 12+ yrs.	6.08		6.08		7.26		6.76		10.03		36.65	
Vs.		2.73**		0.01		0.86		1.63		0.78		1.20
British Girls 12+ yrs.	7.59		5.68		7.49		7.88		9.83		38.53	
British Boys 14+ yrs.	6.59		5.67		7.98		7.04		9.31		35.99	
Vs.		5.23***		0.06		1.43		4.02**		1.96*		4.83***
British Girls 14+ yrs.	9.10		6.06		7.90		8.46		11.14		42.50	

* – 0.05 ** – 0.01 *** – 0.001

Table 4.12 : Significance of the Differences between Means of Sample Groups on EPQ

Sample Groups Compared	*EPQ 'E'*		*EPQ 'N'*		*EPQ 'P'*		*EPQ 'L'*	
	Mean	*CR*	*Mean*	*CR*	*Mean*	*CR*	*Mean*	*CR*
Indian Boys 12+ yrs.	15.38		8.68		5.01		11.66	
Vs.		0.13		1.06		1.38		2.99**
Indian Girls 12+ yrs.	15.95		8.19		3.84		14.55	
Indian Boys 14+ yrs.	16.99		8.60		4.65		12.16	
Vs.		3.59***		0.12		0.32		2.17**
Indian Girls 14+ yrs.	15.24		8.18		4.76		13.13	
British Boys 12+ yrs.	18.78		12.16		4.99		4.79	
Vs.		0.15		2.22*		8.36***		5.79***
British Girls 12+ yrs.	18.72		18.72		2.39		7.48	
British Boys 14+ yrs.	18.88		11.47		4.53		4.99	
Vs.		2.07*		5.19***		4.85***		2.78**
British Girls 14+ yrs.	17.88		17.88		3.00		5.61	

* – 0.05 ** – 0.01 *** – 0.001

No significant correlations are noted between 'P' Score, WNS factors and JEPQ scores for both Indian boys and girls with the exception of 14 years Indian Girls. Only this sample group revealed a negative correlation with Extraversion at 0.05 level.

Western girls ofboth age groups showed more number of positive correlations than boys, between 'P' Score and WNS factors. All the British adolescents reveal significant correlations between 'P' score and Neuroticism factor on JEPQ. However western group girls of 14 years age group differ from others with higher significant level of differences at 0.01. Only 12 years old Western boys show significant correlations of 'P' Score and 'L' Score [Table 4.13 (a) to (e)].

(b) Correlations between 'F' Score and WNS and 'F' Score and Eysenck Personality Questionnaire

Indian adolescents indicate high significant correlation coefficients between 'F' Score and WNS Scores. Only 12 Indian boys differ slightly from the girls showing no significant correlation for IVth factor of WNS (Liability of mood) and relatively lower significant values on factors I (General nematic factor) II (Fear of self-exposure) and III (Uncertainity and social timidity) of WNS.

Indian girls of 14 years old differ from boys by not indicating any significant coefficients between 'F' Score and JEPQ scores. There are significant coefficients observed for 'F' score and psychotism factor in Indian boys sample groups. Negative correlations are observed between 'F" and 'Lie' Scores for Indian adolescents of 12 years old.

The number of positive correlations found between 'F' Score and WNS factors are more for girls than boys. Out of 12 correlations among the four sample groups compared, II were significant for girls groups. The only correlation which was not significant among 14 years girls groups was between 'F' score and WNS factor II (Fear of Self-Exposure).

British boys also reveal seven positive correlations in WNS factors. No significant correlations are indicated between 'F' Score and WNS II factor (Fear of self-exposure) and factor IV (Lability of mood) in British boys sample groups.

Negative correlations co-efficient are noted between 'F' score and Extroversion from EPQ, but the correlation is significant only in case of 12 yrs. British girls. There are positive correlations between 'F' and 'N' Scores of EPQ for all the groups, except for British boys of 14 years.

Positive significant correlations between 'F' Score and psychotism on EPQ is found for only Indian boys of both the age groups. Indian Girls differ from them by not showing any significant correlation co-efficient between 'F' score and 'P' on EPQ scores. Significant, negative correlations is revealed by Indian boys and girls of 12 years age group between 'F' Score and Lie Score on JEPQ. However correlations are not significant in 14 years age groups. Similar results are revealed by Western sample group indicating significant negative correlations by 12 years sample groups of boys and girls. [Table 4.14(a) to (e)].

(C) Scores of WNS Total and JEPQ

All the sample groups show negative correlations between WNS total score and Extraversion on EPQ. However the correlations co-efficient are not significant in 12 years British sample groups. All the girls sample groups reveal significant negative correlation between WNS total score and Extraversion.

Interesting results are noted with regard to WNS total score and ENPL, factors of EPQ.

All the sample groups are found with significant positive correlations between total WNS total score of WNS and Neuroticism. When WNS total score and psychotism scores are studied only Indian boys reveal significant positive correlations between these two at 0.01 level. A negative is found between WNS total score and 'Lie' Score but this is significant only in 14 years Indian and British boys.

Boys have revealed more number (12) of significant correlation coefficients between WNS total score and JEPQ factors than girls (8). Girls do not have significant correlations between WNS total scores and psychotism and Lie Score [Table 4.15 (a) to (e)].

Table 4.13 : PEARSON PRODUCT MOMENT CORRELATIONS FOR 12 YEARS OLD INDIAN GIRLS AND BOYS

Table 4.13(a) : Correlations between 'P' Score and Factors of WNS

Tests Correlated	*Indian Boys 12 years*	*Indian Girls 12 years*
FSS 'P' Score *Vs.* WNS Factor I	0.124	0.318**
FSS 'P' Score *Vs.* WNS Factor II	0.061	0.235**
FSS 'P' Score *Vs.* WNS Factor III	0.095	0.348**
FSS 'P' Score *Vs.* WNS Factor IV	0.004	0.320**
FSS 'P' Score *Vs.* WNS Factor V	0.078	0.303**
FSS 'P' Score *Vs.* WNS Total Score	0.089	0.428**

** – 0.01

Table 4.13(b) : Correlations between 'P' Score and Factors of JEPQ

Tests Correlated	*Indian Boys 12 years*	*Indian Girls 12 years*
FSS 'P' Score *Vs.* EPQ 'E' Score	0.053	0.123
FSS 'P' Score *Vs.* EPQ 'N' Score	0.032	0.153
FSS 'P' Score *Vs.* EPQ 'P' Score		0.080
FSS 'P' Score *Vs.* EPQ 'L' Score	0.012	0.060

Table 4.13(c) : Correlations between 'P' Score and Factors of WNS

Tests Correlated	*Indian Boys 12 years*	*Indian Girls 12 years*
FSS 'P' Score *Vs.* WNS Factor I	0.176	0.284**
FSS 'P' Score *Vs.* WNS Factor II	0.200*	0.251**
FSS 'P' Score *Vs.* WNS Factor III	0.221*	0.314**
FSS 'P' Score *Vs.* WNS Factor IV	0.109	0.290**
FSS 'P' Score *Vs.* WNS Factor V	0.231**	0.320**
FSS 'P' Score *Vs.* WNS Total Score	0.243**	0.407**

* – 0.05 ** – 0.01

Table 4.13(d) : Correlations between 'P' Score and Factors of JEPQ

Tests Correlated	*Indian Boys 12 years*	*Indian Girls 12 years*
FSS 'P' Score *Vs.* EPQ 'E' Score	–0.092	0.179
FSS 'P' Score *Vs.* EPQ 'H' Score	0.151	0.120
FSS 'P' Score *Vs.* EPQ 'P' Score	0.191*	0.010
FSS 'P' Score *Vs.* EPQ 'L' Score	–0.205*	0.514**

* – 0.05 ** – 0.01

Table 4.13(e) : Correlations between WNS Total and Factor of JEPQ

Tests Correlated	*Indian Boys 12 years*	*Indian Girls 12 years*
WNS Total Score *Vs.* EPQ 'E'	–0.229*	–0.188*
WNS Total *Vs.* EPQ 'N'	0.436**	0.325**
WNS Total *Vs.* EPQ 'P'	0.296**	0.075
WNS Total *Vs.* EPQ 'L'	0.375**	0.136

* – 0.05 ** – 0.01

Table 4.14 : PEARSON PRODUCT MOMENT CORRELATIONS FOR 14 YEARS OLD INDIAN GIRLS AND BOYS

Table 4.14(a) : Correlations between 'P' Score and Factors of WNS

Tests Correlated	*Indian Boys 14 years*	*Indian Girls 14 years*
FSS 'P' Score *Vs.* WNS Factor I	0.213*	0.180*
FSS 'P' Score *Vs.* WNS Factor II	0.062	0.200*
FSS 'P' Score *Vs.* WNS Factor III	0.340**	0.121
FSS 'P' Score *Vs.* WNS Factor IV	0.136	0.195*
FSS 'P' Score *Vs.* WNS Factor V	0.171	0.168*
FSS 'P' Score *Vs.* WNS Total Score	0.256**	0.224**

* – 0.05 ** – 0.01

Table 4.14(b) : Correlations between 'P' Score and Factors of JEPQ

Tests Correlated	*Indian Boys 14 years*	*Indian Girls 14 years*
FSS 'P' Score *Vs.* EPQ 'E' Score	−0.137	−0.170*
FSS 'P' Score *Vs.* EPQ 'N' Score	0.013	0.034
FSS 'P' Score *Vs.* EPQ 'P' Score	0.057	0.045
FSS 'P' Score *Vs.* EPQ 'L' Score	−0.058	0.036

* – 0.05

Table 4.14(c) : Correlations between 'P' Score and Factors of WNS

Tests Correlated	*Indian Boys 14 years*	*Indian Girls 14 years*
FSS 'P' Score *Vs.* WNS Factor I	0.311**	0.296**
FSS 'P' Score *Vs.* WNS Factor II	0.238**	0.266**
FSS 'P' Score *Vs.* WNS Factor III	0.410**	0.240**
FSS 'P' Score *Vs.* WNS Factor IV	0.294**	0.230**
FSS 'P' Score *Vs.* WNS Factor V	0.302**	0.248**
FSS 'P' Score *Vs.* WNS Factor Total Score	0.414**	0.335**

* – 0.05 ** – 0.01

Table 4.14(d) : Correlations between 'P' Score and Factors of JEPQ

Tests Correlated	*Indian Boys 14 years*	*Indian Girls 14 years*
FSS 'P' Score *Vs.* EPQ 'E' Score	−0.152	−0.010
FSS 'P' Score *Vs.* EPQ 'N' Score	0.031	0.027
FSS 'P' Score *Vs.* EPQ 'P' Score	0.233**	0.004
FSS 'P' Score *Vs.* EPQ 'L' Score	−0.101	−0.100

** – 0.01

Table 4.14(e) : Correlations between WNS Total and Factor of JEPQ

Tests Correlated	*Indian Boys 14 years*	*Indian Girls 14 years*
WNS Total Score *Vs.* EPQ 'E' Score	–0.338**	–0.238**
WNS Total *Vs.* EPQ 'N' Score	0.272**	0.292**
WNS Total *Vs.* EPQ 'P' Score	0.359**	0.059
WNS Total *Vs.* EPQ 'L' Score	–0.231	–0.079

** – 0.01

Table 4.15 : PEARSON PRODUCT MOMENT CORRELATIONS FOR 12 YEARS OLD BRITISH GIRLS AND BOYS

Table 4.15(a) : Correlations between 'P' Score and Factors of WNS

Tests Correlated	*British Boys 12 years*	*British Girls 12 years*
FSS 'P' Score *Vs.* WNS Factor I	0.180*	0.260**
FSS 'P' Score *Vs.* WNS Factor II	0.037	0.272**
FSS 'P' Score *Vs.* WNS Factor III	0.071	0.225*
FSS 'P' Score *Vs.* WNS Factor IV	0.028	0.221*
FSS 'P' Score *Vs.* WNS Factor V	0.286**	0.314**
FSS 'P' Score *Vs.* WNS Total Score	0.192*	0.328**

* – 0.05 ** – 0.01

Table 4.15(b) : Correlations between 'P' Score and Factors of JEPQ

Tests Correlated	*British Boys 12 years*	*British Girls 12 years*
FSS 'P' Score *Vs.* EPQ 'E' Score	0.090	–0.049
FSS 'P' Score *Vs.* EPQ 'N' Score	0.192*	0.191*
FSS 'P' Score *Vs.* EPQ 'P' Score	0.045	–0.011
FSS 'P' Score *Vs.* EPQ 'L' Score	0.210*	0.170

* – 0.05

Table 4.15(c) : Correlations between 'P' Score and Factors of WNS

Tests Correlated	*British Boys 12 years*	*British Girls 12 years*
FSS 'P' Score *Vs.* WNS Factor I	0.308**	0.331**
FSS 'P' Score *Vs.* WNS Factor II	0.135	0.321**
FSS 'P' Score *Vs.* WNS Factor III	0.193*	0.292**
FSS 'P' Score *Vs.* WNS Factor IV	0.109	0.192*
FSS 'P' Score *Vs.* WNS Factor V	0.312**	0.305**
FSS 'P' Score *Vs.* WNS Total Score	0.304**	0.368**

* – 0.05 ** – 0.01

Table 4.15(d) : Correlations between 'P' Score and Factors of JEPQ

Tests Correlated	*British Boys 12 years*	*British Girls 12 years*
FSS 'P' Score *Vs.* EPQ 'E' Score	–0.080	–0.204*
FSS 'P' Score *Vs.* EPQ 'N' Score	0.288**	–0.248**
FSS 'P' Score *Vs.* EPQ 'P' Score	–0.028	–0.061
FSS 'P' Score *Vs.* EPQ 'L' Score	–0.178*	–0.244**

* – 0.05 ** – 0.01

Table 4.15(e) : Correlations between WNS Total and Factor of JEPQ

Tests Correlated	*British Boys 12 years*	*British Girls 12 years*
WNS Total Score *Vs.* EPQ 'E' Score	–0.096	–0.346**
WNS Total *Vs.* EPQ 'N' Score	0.514**	0.451**
WNS Total *Vs.* EPQ 'P' Score	0.010	0.025
WNS Total *Vs.* EPQ 'L' Score	0.014	0.062

** – 0.01

Table 4.16 : PEARSON PRODUCT MOMENT CORRELATIONS FOR 14 YEARS OLD BRITISH GIRLS AND BOYS

Table 4.16(a) : Correlations between 'P' Score and Factors of WNS

Tests Correlated	*Northern Irish Boys 14 years*	*Northern Irish Girls 14 years*
FSS 'P' Score *Vs.* WNS Factor I	0.272**	0.389**
FSS 'P' Score *Vs.* WNS Factor II	0.117	0.093
FSS 'P' Score *Vs.* WNS Factor III	0.119	0.435**
FSS 'P' Score *Vs.* WNS Factor IV	0.110	0.172
FSS 'P' Score *Vs.* WNS Factor V	0.158*	0.292**
FSS 'P' Score *Vs.* WNS Total Score	0.201*	0.367**

* – 0.05 ** – 0.01

Table 4.16(b) : Correlations between 'P' Score and Factors of JEPQ

Tests Correlated	*Northern Irish Boys 14 years*	*Northern Irish Girls 14 years*
FSS 'P' Score *Vs.* EPQ 'E' Score	0.041	–0.017
FSS 'P' Score *Vs.* EPQ 'N' Score	0.176*	0.313**
FSS 'P' Score *Vs.* EPQ 'P' Score	0.059	–0.048
FSS 'P' Score *Vs.* EPQ 'L' Score	0.088	–0.024

* – 0.05 ** – 0.01

Table 4.16(c) : Correlations between 'P' Score and Factors of WNS

Tests Correlated	*Northern Irish Boys 14 years*	*Northern Irish Girls 14 years*
FSS 'P' Score *Vs.* WNS Factor I	0.348**	0.414**
FSS 'P' Score *Vs.* WNS Factor II	0.027*	0.155
FSS 'P' Score *Vs.* WNS Factor III	0.175*	0.438**
FSS 'P' Score *Vs.* WNS Factor IV	0.169*	0.211*
FSS 'P' Score *Vs.* WNS Factor V	0.158	0.334**
FSS 'P' Score *Vs.* WNS Total Score	0.261**	0.416**

* – 0.05 ** – 0.01

Table 4.16(d) : Correlations between 'P' Score and Factors of JEPQ

Tests Correlated	*Northern Irish Boys 14 years*	*Northern Irish Girls 14 years*
FSS 'P' Score *Vs.* EPQ 'E' Score	–0.002	–0.014
FSS 'P' Score *Vs.* EPQ 'N' Score	0.238**	0.356**
FSS 'P' Score *Vs.* EPQ 'P' Score	–0.022	–0.039
FSS 'P' Score *Vs.* EPQ 'L' Score	–0.002	0.002

* – 0.05 ** – 0.01

Table 4.16(e) : Correlations between WNS Total and Factor of JEPQ

Tests Correlated	*Northern Irish Boys 14 years*	*Northern Irish Girls 14 years*
WNS Total Score *Vs.* EPQ 'E'	–0.294**	0.204*
WNS Total *Vs.* EPQ 'N' Score	0.528**	0.573**
WNS Total *Vs.* EPQ 'P' Score	0.059	–0.079
WNS Total *Vs.* EPQ 'L' Score	–0.232**	0.055

* – 0.05 ** – 0.01

Section —3

This section of results contain the nationality differences by comparing the Indian and British sample groups on the tests administered the findings are presented as follows:

1. AH_4 Intelligence (AH_4).
2. 'P' and 'F' scores of FSS.
3. Willoughby Neuroticism Schedule.
4. Junior Eysenck Personality Questionnaire.
5. Correlation comparison by Nationality.

Findings on Nationality Differences

The most prominent feature of emerge from the examination of the significant of differences of all sample groups between all tests is, the complete uniformity within the Indian and British sample groups. The level of significance for all the sample groups is same (*i.e.* P 0.001). The differences are highly significant as the level of significance is at P 0.001.

Differences in Intelligence

AH_4 Intelligence (AH_4) Test

There are consistent significant differences on mean scores for both the nationality groups (Table 1(a), 1(b), 1(c). Indian adolescents of all sample groups have lower mean scores on all the parts of AH_4 Intelligence Test. British adolescent sample groups differed significantly from Indian adolescent sample groups with higher mean scores on all parts of the AH_4 Intelligence (Table 4.17).

Table 4.17 : Significance of the Differences between Means by Sample Groups on AH_4 Intelligence Test

Sample Groups Compared	*Verbal*		*Non-verbal*		*Total*	
	Mean	*CR*	*Mean*	*CR*	*Mean*	*CR*
Indian Boys 12 yrs.	31.98		38.35		70.25	
Vs.		7.49***		6.97***		8.15***
British Boys 12 yrs.	41.18		48.58		89.84	
Indian Boys 14 yrs.	38.52		44.55		83.08	
Vs.		9.64***		11.16***		11.99***
British Boys 14 yrs.	48.07		55.56		103.62	
Indian Girls 12 yrs.	28.02		31.48		59.14	
Vs.		9.06***		8.84***		9.94***
British Girls 12 yrs.	38.45		43.49		81.94	
Indian Girls 14 yrs.	30.12		35.80		65.99	
Vs.		14.56***		11.86***		14.14***
British Girls 14 yrs.	49.33		52.46		10.74	

*** – 0.001

Comparison of Phobias and Fears

'P' and 'F' Scores on Fear Survey Schedule

Indian sample groups have higher 'P' and 'F' mean scores on all the significant differences (Table 4.1). Indian and British boys and girls of 12 years. age groups do not differ significantly on 'P' scores while 14 years sample, groups differ significantly on 'P' scores. Indian boys and girls of 14 years age group differ with higher mean on 'P' score. British sample groups differ from Indian sample groups significantly with lower means on 'F' scores (Table 4.18).

Table 4.18 : Significance of the Differences between Means by Sample Groups on FSS

Sample Groups Compared	*FSS 'P' Score*		*FSS 'F' Score*	
	Mean	*CR*	*Mean*	*CR*
Indian Boys 12 yrs.	10.99		120.14	
Vs.		1.84		4.62***
British Boys 12 yrs.	8.24		85.55	
Indian Boys 14 yrs.	14.53		138.39	
Vs.		8.32***		7.05***
British Boys 14 yrs.	6.81		85.65	
Indian Girls 12 yrs.	17.14		149.12	
Vs.		1.18		2.11*
British Girls 12 yrs.	15.35		131.11	
Indian Girls 14 yrs.	18.09		159.53	
Vs.		2.27*		2.21*
British Girls 14 yrs.	14.57		140.50	

* - 0.05 ** - 0.01 *** - 0.001

Differences in Neuroticism

Willoughby Neuroticism Schedule (WNS)

British sample groups have higher mean scores on all the significant differences of factors of Willoughby Neuroticism Schedule (Table 1(d), (Table 4.2). The mean scores which are not significantly different are more confined to boys groups then girls groups accounting for four differences out of five cases of significant differences. There is only one negative score between Indian girls of 14 years and British girls of 14 years age. They do not differ in uncertainty and social timidity (III factor) which indicates that there is no significant difference of nationality between these sample groups on this factor. There are significant differences between British and Indian groups on the mean scores of lability of mood (IV factor) and total score of WNS. British boys and girls sample groups significantly differ in these factors with higher mean scores than the mean scores of Indian girls and boys.

Boys of 12 years, age groups do not differ accounting to nationality on the factor of general neurotic factor (I factor) and lack of self-confidence and social inadequacy (V factor). There were no significant nationality differences on the general neurotic factor (I factor) and uncertainity and social timidly (III factor) between Indian and British sample group of 14 years age groups boys (Table 4.19).

Personality Differences

Eysenck Personality Questionnaire (JEPQ)

Clear trends are found with Extraversion, Neurotics, psychotism and lie-scale of JEPQ between the two sample groups. Out of sixteen mean scores compared only two are not significantly different which are confined to boys sample groups (Table 4.3). On both Extraversion and Neuroticism British sample groups show higher mean scores than Indian sample groups while on Psychotism and Lie score Indian sample groups have higher mean scores than British sample groups. Indian girls indicate higher mean scores on psychotism than British girls. The only factor of JEPQ on which boys do not show significant differences is psychotism (Table 4.20).

(a) Correlations between 'P' Scores and WNS and 'P' scores and JEPQ Scores

With an exception of Indian boys of 12 years old, all the adolescents indicate significant correlations, between 'P' Score and WNS factors. The number of significant correlations are more for both Indian and British Girls, than Boys. An interesting finding is observed

Table 4.19 : Significance of the Differences between Means of Indian and British Adolescents on WNS

Sample Groups Compared	WNS FI		WNS FII		WNS FIII		WNS FIV		WNS FV		WNS Total	
	Mean	CR	Mean	CR	Mean	CR	Mean	CR	Mean	CR	Mean	CR
Indian Boys 12 yrs.	6.30		4.24		7.09		5.01		8.27		30.56	
Vs.		0.41		3.43***		6.51***		3.90***		11.60		2.60**
British Boys 12 yrs.	6.08		6.08		7.26		6.76		10.03		36.65	
Indian Boys 14 yrs.	6.05		4.26		6.55		4.58		6.99		28.38	
Vs.		1.14		5.65***		1.47		5.34***		4.48***		4.63***
British Boys 14 yrs.	6.59		5.67		7.98		7.04		9.31		35.99	
Indian Girls 12 yrs.	5.57		2.94		6.27		3.57		6.09		24.43	
Vs.		3.58***		7.43***		2.33*		8.68***		5.98***		7.20***
British Girls 12 yrs.	7.59		5.68		7.49		7.88		9.83		38.53	
Indian Girls 14 yrs.	6.12		4.01		7.21		4.65		7.44		29.44	
Vs.		5.66***		5.67***		1.43		8.19***		5.89***		6.91***
British Girls 14 yrs.	9.10		6.06		7.90		8.46		11.14		42.50	

** – 0.01 *** – 0.001

Table 4.20 : Significance of the Difference between Means of Indian and British Adolescents on JEPQ

Sample Groups Compared	*JEPQ 'E'*		*JEPQ 'N'*		*JEPQ 'P'*		*JEPQ 'L'*	
	Mean	*CR*	*Mean*	*CR*	*Mean*	*CR*	*Mean*	*CR*
Indian Boys 12 yrs.	15.38		8.68		5.01		11.66	
Vs.		6.71***		7.44***		0.04		15.07***
British Boys 12 yrs.	18.78		12.16		4.99		4.79	
Indian Boys 14 yrs.	16.99		8.59		4.65		12.16	
Vs.		4.63***		3.97***		0.38		18.49***
British Boys 14 yrs.	18.88		11.47		4.53		4.99	
Indian Girls 12 yrs.	15.95		8.19		3.84		14.55	
Vs.		6.13***		10.70***		5.56***		15.58***
British Girls 12 yrs.	18.72		18.72		2.39		7.48	
Indian Girls 14 yrs.	15.24		8.18		4.76		13.13	
Vs.		5.14***		12.06***		5.21***		16.94***
British Girls 14 yrs.	17.88		17.88		3.00		5.61	

*** – 0.001

with British adolescents. All the British adolescents sample groups reveal a positive significant correlation between 'P' Score and Neuroticism factor on JEPQ Questionnaire. The only sample group which has revealed a positive significant correlation between 'P' score and Lie score of JEPQ is British boys of 12 years old. (Table 4.21 (a) and (b), 4.22(a) and (b), 4.23(a) and (b) and 4.24(a) and (b)).

Indian sample groups do not reveal any significant correlations between 'P' Score and factors of JEPQ Scores. However Indian Girls of 14 years old show a negative correlation between 'P' Score and Extraversion Score on JEPQ Questionnaire. This is significant at the level of 0.05.

(b) Correlations between 'F' Scores and WNS and 'F' Score and Junior Eysenck personality Questionnaire

All the sample groups show significant positive correlations between 'F' Score and WNS factors. However the number of correlations are more in Indian Samples. The only factor of WNS which correlates significantly with 'F' Score, for all the sample groups is Factor III (Uncertainity and Social Timidity).

A negative correlation is found between 'F' Scores and Extraversion. The Correlation Co-efficients reach significant level in case of 14 years British Girls, 12 years Indian and British Girls. Indian adolescent differ from British adolescents by not revealing significant correlations between 'F' Score and neuroticism factor on JEPQ.

Indian boys differ from British boys indicating significant correlations between 'F' Scores and Psychotism factor on JEPQ. Girls sample groups of both the nations do not show any significant differences (Table 4.21 (c), (d), 4.22(c) and (d), 4.23(c) and (d) and 4.24 (c) and (d).

Only one pair of sample groups reveal significant correlations between 'F' Score and Lie Score. *i.e.* 12 years old boys of both the nations do not differ in the correlations between 'F' Scores and Lie Score. Both the groups show significant correlations at 0.05 level. Other sample groups do not reveal any nationality difference between 'F' Score and Lie Score. There are more similarities than differences.

(c) Scores of WNS and JEPQ

Indian boys and obtain significant correlations between WNS

Scores and all the factors of JEPQ. The correlations is negative between WNS total score and Extraversion and Lie Score for these sample groups. Similarity the correlations are significant between WNS total Score and Extraversion and Neurotism, for Indian and British Girls of 12 years and 14 years old groups.

Indian sample groups have revealed more number of significant correlation coefficients (12) compared to British sample groups between WNS total Score and JEPQ factors.

With the exception of 14 years British boys, there are no significant correlations between WNS total Score and Psychotism and Lie Scores of British sample groups. 14 years British boys show significant negative correlation between WNS total Score and Lie Score on EPQ.

Indian boys of 12 years old has significant correlation coefficients between WNS total score and 'P' score and 'L' score on JEPQ, while the British boys of same age group do not reveal significant correlations, on these factors.

All the girls groups do not indicate any significant correlation between WNS and 'P' and 'L' scores on EPQ. (Table 4.21(e), 4.22(e),

Table 4.21 : PEARSON PRODUCT MOMENT CORRELATIONS FOR 12 YEARS OLD INDIAN AND BRITISH GIRLS

Table 4.21(a) : Correlations between 'P' Score and Factors of WNS

Tests Correlated	*Indian Grils 12 years*	*British Girls 12 years*
FSS 'P' Score *Vs.* WNS Factor I	0.318**	0.260**
FSS 'P' Score *Vs.* WNS Factor II	0.235**	0.272**
FSS 'P' Score *Vs.* WNS Factor III	0.348**	0.225*
FSS 'P' Score *Vs.* WNS Factor IV	0.320**	0.221*
FSS 'P' Score *Vs.* WNS Factor V	0.303**	0.314**
FSS 'P' Score *Vs.* WNS Total Score	0.428**	0.328**

* – 0.05 ** – 0.01

Table 4.21(b) : Correlations between 'P' Score and Factors of JEPQ

Tests Correlated	*Indian Grils 12 years*	*British Girls 12 years*
FSS 'P' Score *Vs.* JEPQ 'E' Score	0.123	0.049
FSS 'P' Score *Vs.* JEPQ 'N' Score	0.153	0.191
FSS 'P' Score *Vs.* JEPQ 'P' Score	0.080	0.011*
FSS 'P' Score *Vs.* JEPQ 'L' Score	0.060	0.170

* – 0.05

Table 4.21(c) : Correlations between 'F' Score and Factors of WNS

Tests Correlated	*Indian Grils 12 years*	*British Girls 12 years*
FSS 'F' Score *Vs.* WNS Factor I	0.284**	0.331**
FSS 'F' Score *Vs.* WNS Factor II	0.251**	0.321**
FSS 'F' Score *Vs.* WNS Factor III	0.314**	0.292**
FSS 'F' Score *Vs.* WNS Factor IV	0.290**	0.192*
FSS 'F' Score *Vs.* WNS Factor V	0.320**	0.305**
FSS 'F' Score *Vs.* WNS Total Score	0.407**	0.368**

* – 0.05 ** – 0.01

Table 4.21(d) : Correlations between 'P' Score and Factors of JEPQ

Tests Correlated	*Indian Grils 12 years*	*British Girls 12 years*
FSS 'P' Score *Vs.* JEPQ 'E' Score	0.179*	0.204*
FSS 'P' Score *Vs.* JEPQ 'N' Score	0.120	0.248**
FSS 'P' Score *Vs.* JEPQ 'P' Score	0.010	0.061
FSS 'P' Score *Vs.* JEPQ 'L' Score	0.514	0.244

* – 0.05 ** – 0.01

Table 4.21(e) : Correlations and JEPQ between WNS Total

Tests Correlated	*Indian Grils 12 years*	*British Girls 12 years*
WNS Total *Vs.* JEPQ 'E'	0.188*	–0.348**
WNS Total *Vs.* JEPQ 'N'	0.324**	0.451**
WNS Total *Vs.* JEPQ 'P'	0.075	–0.025
WNS Total *Vs.* JEPQ 'L'	0.136	–0.062

* – 0.05 ** – 0.01

Table 4.22 : PEARSON PRODUCT MOMENT CORRELATIONS FOR 14 YEARS OLD INDIAN AND BRITISH GIRLS

Table 4.22(a) : Correlations between 'P' Score and Factors of WNS

Tests Correlated	*Indian Girls 14 years*	*Northern Irish Girls 14 years*
FSS 'F' Score *Vs.* WNS Factor I	0.180*	0.389**
FSS 'P' Score *Vs.* WNS Factor II	0.200*	0.093
FSS 'P' Score *Vs.* WNS Factor III	0.121	0.435**
FSS 'P' Score *Vs.* WNS Factor IV	0.195*	0.172
FSS 'P' Score *Vs.* WNS Factor V	0.168*	0.292**
FSS 'P' Score *Vs.* WNS Total Score	0.224**	0.367**

* – 0.05 ** – 0.01

Table 4.22(b) : Correlations between 'P' Score and Factors of JEPQ

Tests Correlated	*Indian Grils 14 years*	*Northern Irish Girls 14 years*
FSS 'P' Score *Vs.* JEPQ 'E' Score	0.170*	0.017
FSS 'P' Score *Vs.* JEPQ 'N' Score	0.034	0.313**
FSS 'P' Score *Vs.* JEPQ 'P' Score	0.045	0.048
FSS 'P' Score *Vs.* JEPQ 'L' Score	0.036	0.024

* – 0.05 ** – 0.01

Table 4.22(c) : Correlations between 'F' Score and Factors of WNS

Tests Correlated	*Indian Girls 14 years*	*Northern Irish Girls 14 years*
FSS 'F' Score *Vs.* WNS Factor I	0.296**	0.414**
FSS 'F' Score *Vs.* WNS Factor II	0.266**	0.155
FSS 'F' Score *Vs.* WNS Factor III	0.240**	0.438**
FSS 'F' Score *Vs.* WNS Factor IV	0.230**	0.211*
FSS 'F' Score *Vs.* WNS Factor V	0.248**	0.334**
FSS 'F' Score *Vs.* WNS Total Score	0.335*	0.416**

* – 0.05 ** – 0.01

Table 4.21(d) : Correlations between 'E' Score and Factors of JEPQ

Tests Correlated	*Indian Girls 14 years*	*Northern Irish Girls 14 years*
FSS 'F' Score *Vs.* JEPQ 'E' Score	0.010	0.014**
FSS 'F' Score *Vs.* JEPQ 'N' Score	0.027	0.356**
FSS 'F' Score *Vs.* JEPQ 'P' Score	0.004	0.039
FSS 'F' Score *Vs.* JEPQ 'L' Score	0.110	0.002

** – 0.01

Table 4.22(e) : Correlations between WNS Total and Factor of JEPQ

Tests Correlated	*Indian Girls 14 years*	*Northern Irish Girls 14 years*
WNS Total *Vs.* JEPQ 'E'	–0.238**	0.204*
WNS Total *Vs.* JEPQ 'N'	0.292**	0.573**
WNS Total *Vs.* JEPQ 'P'	0.059	–0.079
WNS Total *Vs.* JEPQ 'L'	–0.079	0.055

* – 0.05 ** – 0.01

Table 4.23 : PEARSON PRODUCT MOMENT CORRELATIONS FOR 12 YEARS OLD INDIAN AND BRITISH GIRLS

Table 4.23(a) : Correlations between 'P' Score and Factors of WNS

Tests Correlated	*Indian Boys 12 years*	*British Boys 12 years*
FSS 'P' Score *Vs.* WNS Factor I	0.124	0.180*
FSS 'P' Score *Vs.* WNS Factor II	0.061	0.037
FSS 'P' Score *Vs.* WNS Factor III	0.095	0.071
FSS 'P' Score *Vs.* WNS Factor IV	–0.004	0.028
FSS 'P' Score *Vs.* WNS Factor V	0.078	0.286**
FSS 'P' Score *Vs.* WNS Total Score	0.089	0.192*

* – 0.05 ** – 0.01

Table 4.23(b) : Correlations between 'P' Score and Factors of JEPQ

Tests Correlated	*Indian Boys 12 years*	*British Boys 12 years*
FSS 'P' Score *Vs.* JEPQ 'E' Score	0.053	0.09
FSS 'P' Score *Vs.* JEPQ 'N' Score	–0.032	0.192*
FSS 'P' Score *Vs.* JEPQ 'P' Score	0.000	0.045
FSS 'P' Score *Vs.* JEPQ 'L' Score	–0.012	0.210*

* – 0.05

Table 4.23(c) : Correlations between 'F' Score and Factors of WNS

Tests Correlated	*Indian Boys 12 years*	*British Boys 12 years*
FSS 'F' Score *Vs.* WNS Factor I	0.176*	0.308**
FSS 'F' Score *Vs.* WNS Factor II	0.200*	0.135
FSS 'F' Score *Vs.* WNS Factor III	0.221*	0.193*
FSS 'F' Score *Vs.* WNS Factor IV	0.109	0.109
FSS 'F' Score *Vs.* WNS Factor V	0.231**	0.312***
FSS 'F' Score *Vs.* WNS Total Score	0.243	0.304

* – 0.05 ** – 0.01

Table 4.23(d) : Correlations between 'F' Score and Factors of JEPQ

Tests Correlated	*Indian Boys 12 years*	*Northern Irish Boys 12 years*
FSS 'F' Score *Vs.* JEPQ 'E' Score	0.092	–0.080**
FSS 'F' Score *Vs.* JEPQ 'N' Score	0.151	0.288**
FSS 'F' Score *Vs.* JEPQ 'P' Score	0.191*	–0.028
FSS 'F' Score *Vs.* JEPQ 'L' Score	0.205*	0.178*

* – 0.05 ** – 0.01

Table 4.23(e) : Correlations between WNS Total and Factor of JEPQ

Tests Correlated	*Indian Boys 12 years*	*British Boys 12 years*
WNS Total *Vs.* JEPQ 'E'	0.229*	–0.096
WNS Total *Vs.* JEPQ 'N'	0.436**	0.514**
WNS Total *Vs.* JEPQ 'P'	0.296**	0.101
WNS Total *Vs.* JEPQ 'L'	0.375**	–0.014

* – 0.05 ** – 0.01

Table 4.24 : PEARSON PRODUCT MOMENT CORRELATIONS FOR 14 YEARS OLD INDIAN AND BRITISH BOYS

Table 4.24(a) : Correlations between 'P' Score and Factors of WNS

Tests Correlated	*Indian Boys 14 years*	*Northern Irish Boys 14 years*
FSS 'P' Score *Vs.* WNS Factor I	0.213*	0.272**
FSS 'P' Score *Vs.* WNS Factor II	0.062	0.117
FSS 'P' Score *Vs.* WNS Factor III	0.340**	0.119
FSS 'P' Score *Vs.* WNS Factor IV	0.136	0.110
FSS 'P' Score *Vs.* WNS Factor V	0.171	0.158*
FSS 'P' Score *Vs.* WNS Total Score	0.256**	0.201*

* – 0.05 ** – 0.01

Table 4.24(b) : Correlations between 'P' Score and Factors of JEPQ

Tests Correlated	*Indian Boys 14 years*	*Northern Irish Boys 14 years*
FSS 'P' Score *Vs.* JEPQ 'E' Score	0.137	0.041
FSS 'P' Score *Vs.* JEPQ 'N' Score	0.013	0.176*
FSS 'P' Score *Vs.* JEPQ 'P' Score	0.057	0.059
FSS 'P' Score *Vs.* JEPQ 'L' Score	0.059	0.088

* – 0.05

Table 4.24(c) : Correlations between 'F' Score and Factors of WNS

Tests Correlated	*Indian Boys 14 years*	*Northern Irish Boys 14 years*
FSS 'F' Score *Vs.* WNS Factor I	0.311**	0.348
FSS 'F' Score *Vs.* WNS Factor II	0.238**	0.207*
FSS 'F' Score *Vs.* WNS Factor III	0.416**	0.175*
FSS 'F' Score *Vs.* WNS Factor IV	0.294**	0.169*
FSS 'F' Score *Vs.* WNS Factor V	0.302**	0.158
FSS 'F' Score *Vs.* WNS Total Score	0.414**	0.261

* – 0.05 ** – 0.01

Table 4.24(d) : Correlations between 'P' Score and Factors of JEPQ

Tests Correlated	*Indian Boys 14 years*	*Northern Irish Boys 14 years*
FSS 'F' Score *Vs.* JEPQ 'E' Score	0.152	0.002
FSS 'F' Score *Vs.* JEPQ 'N' Score	0.031	0.238
FSS 'F' Score *Vs.* JEPQ 'P' Score	0.233**	0.022
FSS 'F' Score *Vs.* JEPQ 'L' Score	0.101	0.002

** – 0.01

Table 4.24(e) : Correlations between WNS Total and Factor of JEPQ

Tests Correlated	*Indian Boys 14 years*	*Northern Irish Boys 14 years*
WNS Total *Vs.* JEPQ 'E'	0.338**	0.294**
WNS Total *Vs.* JEPQ 'N'	0.272**	0.528**
WNS Total *Vs.* JEPQ 'P'	0.359**	0.059
WNS Total *Vs.* JEPQ 'L'	–0.231**	0.232**

** – 0.01

4.23(e) and 4.24(e).

PART — II

Section — 1

Items on FSS Compared on the Basis of the Means and Standard Deviations of their 'F' Scores

The present analysis investigates variations in the mean scores of items on FSS in terms of the variables of age, gender and nationality differences.

The score given to each item on FSS were separately summed up for boys and girls at each sample group. The means and standard deviations of these item F scores were then computated. Appendix 4(a) and (c) present item means and critical ratios for both the Indian and British sample groups. The significant differences are indicated by asterick in these appendixes. The significance of the differences between means was ascertained by using Fisher's 't' test. The Appendixes 4(a), and (b) and (c) give the significant differences of items on FSS by age, gender nationality differences.

(a) Age differences

When count is made, for all the sample groups for significant differences, the greatest number of such differences was found in British girls of 12 and 14 years old (22 significant differences) and between Indian girls group of 12 years and 14 years (20 significant differences).

There are also certain trends within the total number of significant differences. 14 years age group had more number of items having higher mean scores when compared with 12 years age groups, with an exception of British boys groups where 12 years age group has more number of items with higher mean score to that of 14 years age group.

Indian girls of 14 years old group has significantly higher mean scores on the following items compared to 12 years Indian girls.

(1) Feeling angry
(2) People in authority
(3) Crowds
(4) Journey by bus
(5) Mice or rats
(6) Feeling rejected by others
(7) Doctors
(8) Harmless spiders
(9) Dogs
(10) Drugs
(11) Open doors or windows
(12) Pregnancy
(13) Thoughts of being sexually assaulted
(14) Marriage
(15) Teachers
(16) Unemployment.

The 12 years Indian girls have significantly higher mean scores on following items as compared to 14 years Indian girls.

(1) Dentists
(2) Being watched working
(3) Feeling disapproval of
(4) Cemeteries

Indian boys of 14 years age group has 17 significantly higher mean scores on the following items compared to 12 years Indian boys.

(1) Being alone
(2) Loud voices
(3) Being teased
(4) Making mistakes

(5) Thoughts of being mentally ill
(6) Being ugly
(7) Being punished by god
(8) Being dominated by others
(9) Loss of loved ones
(10) Ministers or priests
(11) Laughing or crying uncontrollably
(12) Being ignored
(13) Leaving the inflammable gas on
(14) Buildings where someone has died
(15) Feeling disapproval of
(16) Going alone into a dark theatre
(17) Unemployment.

The 12 years Indian boys have significantly higher mean scores on the following items as compared to 14 years Indian boys.

(1) Failures
(2) Thieves.

British girls of 14 years age group has greater number of items with significantly higher mean scores on the following items as compared to 12 years British girls.

(1) Travelling
(2) Failures
(3) Bats
(4) Dirt
(5) Seeing a fight
(6) Fire
(7) Being criticized
(8) Angry people
(9) Feeling rejected by others
(10) Medical odours
(11) Feeling disapproval
(12) Being ignored
(13) Loss of loved one

(14) Hurting others.

The 12 years British girls have significantly higher mean scores on the following items as compared to 14 years British girls.

(1) Journeys by care
(2) The heart missing a beat
(3) Living away from family
(4) Physical examination
(5) Thought of having a defective child
(6) Marriage
(7) Teachers
(8) Thieves

British boys 12 years age group has significantly higher mean scores on the following items as compared to 14 years British boys.

(1) Dead people
(2) Fire
(3) Being seen unclothed
(4) Drugs
(5) Buildings where someone had died
(6) Thought of having a defective child
(7) Going alone into a dark theatre
(8) Teachers
(9) Unemployment.

The 14 years British boys have significantly higher mean scores on the following items compared to 12 years British boys.

(1) Speaking in public
(2) Travelling
(3) Entering a room where other people are already seated.
(4) Crawling insects.

(b) Gender Differences

As has already been mentioned item means and critical ratios for both boys and girls samples are set out along side in tables Appendix-4(a), (b) and (c). In all the sample groups it was found that girls have more number of items which have significantly higher mean scores.

If a count is made of the items on which the girls' sample has significantly higher mean scores in all sample groups, the following items and totals are obtained, classified into Wolpe/Lang categories:

(1) **Animal** (2 items) — Flying insects, insecticides.

(2) **Classical Phobias** (2 items) — Being alone, Going alone into a dark theatre.

(3) **Miscellaneous** (2 items) — Strange shapes, pregnancy.

(4) **Noise** (1 item) — Thunder.

(5) **Social Stimuli** (4 items) — Being watched working, being touched by others, Being with a member of the opposite sex, Kissing.

(6) **Tissue Damage** (5 items) — People who seem insane, Receiving injections, Doctors, Thoughts of being sexually assaulted, Thoughts of having a defective child.

Thus in only one category (Tissue damage) to girls have more than 1% of the items with means significantly higher than those for boys in all sample groups.

The boys and girls samples can be compared by summing up for each sample group, the number of items on which girls have significantly higher means than boys; the number of items on which boys have significantly higher mean scores than girls and the number of items on which there is no significant difference between means. The total arrived at are given in Table 4.25.

Table 4.25

Sample Group	*No. of items on which girls have significantly higher means*	*No. of items on which boys have significantly higher means*	*No. of items on which differences between means not significant*
12 yrs. Indian Girls *Vs.* 12 yrs. Indian Boys	42	8	61
14 yrs. Indian Girls *Vs.* 14 yrs. Indian Boys	40	2	69
12 yrs. British Girls *Vs.* 12 yrs. British Boys	68	1	42
14 yrs. British Girls *Vs.* 14 yrs. British Boys	80	2	29

Considering all sample groups it can be observed from the above table that 14years British girls sample has more number of items which have higher significant means.

(c) Nationality Difference

When all sample groups were compared, it was observed that the Indian sample groups has greater number of items with higher mean scores with are significant.

The greatest number (79) of significant differences was found in 14 years boys groups.

The Indian and British sample groups can be compared by summing for each sample group, the number of items on which Indian sample groups have significantly higher means than British sample groups. The Table 4.26 shows the nationality differences.

Table 4.26

Sample Group	*No. of items on which Indian have significantly higher means*	*No. of items on which British have significantly higher means*	*No. of items on which differences between means not significant*
12 yrs. Indian Girls *Vs.* 12 yrs. British Girls	45	15	51
14 yrs. Indian Girls *Vs.* 14 yrs. British Girls	45	18	48
12 yrs. Indian Boys *Vs.* 12 yrs British Boys	65	6	40
14 yrs. Indian Boys *Vs* 14 yrs. British Boys	77	3	31

When a count is made of the items on which the Indian and British samples have significantly higher mean scores in all sample groups, the following items and totals are obtained, classified into Wolps/Lang categories:

Indian Adolescents

(1) **Animal** (4 items) — Cats, birds, crawling insects, dogs.

(2) **Classical Phobias** (2 items) — Being alone, crossing

streets, motor cars, journeys by train, journeys by car, sight of deep water, journeys by bus, large open spaces, living outside door unlocked, open door or windows, leaving away from family.

(3) **Miscellaneous** (4 items) — being a strange place, failure, imaginary creatures, making mistakes.

(4) **Noise** (2 items) — Loud voices, sirens

(5) **Social Stimuli** (7 items) — strangers, crowds, ugly people, being touched by others, angry people, being with a member of opposite sex, Kissing.

(6) **Tissue damage** (2 items) — Becoming giddy, sight of knives or sharp objects.

British Adolescents

(1) **Animal** (4 items) — Mice or rats, Harmless spiders, Bats, Crawling insects.

(2) **Classifiable Phobias** (4 items) — Dirt, fire, lightening, crossing streets.

(3) **Miscellaneous** (3 items) — Taking written tests, pregnancy, unemployment.

(4) **Noise** — Nil.

(5) **Social Stimuli** (6 items) — Feeling disapproved of, giving off an offensive odour, loss of loved one, physical examination, feeling rejected by others, speaking in public.

(6) **Tissue damage** (10 items) — Dead animals, thoughts of being mentally ill, drugs, thoughts of being sexually assaulted, thought of having defective child, dead people, dentists, witnessing surgical operations, being ugly and procpect of a eurgical operation.

Table 4.27

Animal		*Classical Phobia*		*Miscella-neous*		*Noise*		*Social*		*Tissue Damage*	
I	*B*	*I*	*B*	*I*	*B*	*I*	*B*	*I*	*B*	*I*	*B*
4	4	11	4	4	3	2	0	7	6	2	10

I = Indian B = British

Indian adolescents have more number of classical fears, while the British adolescents have more number of fear items in tissue damage category.

Section — 2

Top Twelve Phobic Fears

This section is concerned with those items in the FSS which subjects had placed in the column needed 'very much' and on which the P score is based. The percentage of registration of individual items on FSS described here refers to percentage of subjects who chose to place the items on FSS in this column *i.e.* as 'very much'.

Table I describes the top twelve fears of total sample (521 girls and 543 boys) studied in rank order of percentage. Table II gives the percentage frequency of all fears (phobic) on FSS for each sample group. Table I and II examine for each sample group those items which are ranked in the top twelve positions.

The percentage range of items appearing in the top twelve for each sample group are as follows:

British Boys :

At 12 years	:	Loss of loved one (44%) to	(Rank 1)
		Being ugly (16%)	(Rank 12)
At 14 years	:	Loss of loved one (35%) to	(Rank 1)
		Prospect of surgical operation (14%)	(Rank 12)

Indian Boys :

At 12 years	:	Failure (42%) to	(Rank 1)
		Feeling rejected by others being ugly (16.8)	(Rank 12)
At 14 years	:	Failure (50%) to	(Rank 1)
		Being ugly (21.6%)	(Rank 12)

British Girls :

At 12 years	:	Thoughts of being sexually assaulted (56%) to	(Rank 1)
		Being punished by God (32%)	(Rank 12)
At 14 years	:	Loss of loved one (68%) to	(Rank 1)
		Being punished by god leaving inflammable gas on (28.0%)	(Rank 12)

<u>Indian Girls</u> :

At 12 years	:	Failure (42%) to		(Rank 1)
		Being ugly Thought of having a defective child Loss of loved one The heart missing a best	28%	(Rank 12)
At 14 years	:	Being punished by God (51%) to		(Rank 1)
		Going into a dark theatre Dead people Buildings where some has died Leaving the inflammable gas on	29%	(Rank 12)

Further examination of the table produces the following comparisons.

1. Being seen unclothed
   Dead people
   Thought of having a defective child

2. Being punished by god
   Loss of loved one

3. Unemployment
   Being ugly
   Thoughts of suicide

Age Difference

The top twelve fears of 12 years and 14 years sample groups of Indian and British adolescents were given in Table III. The differences in the percentage range of top twelve fears for 12 years lies between

40.6% to 15.67% and 52.1% to 16.7% for 14 years sample group. In case of 14 years age group the percentage range is slightly greater for both boys and girls (Table III).

Table IV and Table V give the top twelve fears on FSS classified according to the scheme adopted by Wolpe and Lang. The percentage of distribution between the two age group was as follows:

Table 4.28

	12 years	*14 years*
Animal	1	1
Classical	2	1
Miscellaneous	10	2
Social stimuli	12	15
Tissue damage	25	22

Gender Differences

Girls scored greater percentage in top twelve fears than boys. (Table III) (a) and (b). The number of fear items shared are more than the number of items unique to the sample groups.

Classification of fears on Wolpe and Lang category brought out certain gender differences in top twelve fears.

Table 4.29

	Boys	*Girls*
Animal	0	2
Classical	0	3
Miscellaneous	12	9
Social stimuli	13	11
Tissue damage	23	24

Boys did not report fears of animals and classicable types while girls reported them. Table IV and V give the percentages of top twelve fears on Wolpe and Lang classification.

Nationality Differences

On the FSS the effect of this third variable could be clearly noted with the comparison of girls and boys than between the age groups. Table I gives the top twelve fears of Indian and British adolescents with percentages. There were equal number of items 30% and above for both the age groups.

Further examine of Table III (a) and (b) give the following nationality comparison.

<u>Phobic Score Items in Top Twelve Shared by All British Adolescents:</u>

Thoughts of having a defective child Drugs Thoughts of being mentally ill	For both male and female samples
Mice/rats Giving off an offensive odour Thoughts of being sexually assaulted	All female sample
Thoughts of having a defective child Prospect of a surgical operation	All male samples

<u>Phobic Scoring Items in Top Twelve Shared by Indian Adolescents:</u>

Failure Thoughts of suicide	Both male and female samples
Ghosts Living away from family The heart missing a beat Building where someone has died	All female samples
Feeing rejected by others Hurting others	All male samples

Table VI shows Nationality differences among the various sample groups. It was found that there was significant differences between the Indian and British nationality only in 12 years girls at 0.05 level. (Table 4.34).

Table 4.30 : Top Twelve Phobic Fears of Indian and British Adolescents

	Indian Adolescents	*%age*	*British Adolescents*	*%age*
#1.	Failure	43.7	Loss of loved one	50.4
2.	Being punished by God	41.4	*Thoughts of being sexually assaulted	34.6
3.	Being seen unclothed	34.2	Thoughts of having a defective child	32.3
4.	Loss of loved one	34.0	*Thoughts of being mentally ill	33.5
5.	Thoughts of suicide	29.3	Being punished by God	29.3
#6.	Ghosts	26.2	Being seen unclothed	28.5
7.	Dead people	26.2	*Drugs	28.3
8.	Unemployment	25.1	Dead people	26.2
#9.	Hurting Others	24.5	Thoughts of suicide	24.3
#10.	Living away from family	24.3	*Giving off an offensive odour	22.8
#11.	The heart missing a beat	24.1	*Witnessing surgical operation	22.8
12.	Thought of having a defective child	23.8	Unemployment *Being ugly	22.4 22.4

* items unique to each group.

Table 4.31 : Top Twelve Phobic Fears

		12 Years				*14 Years*			
		Indian		*British*		*Indian*		*British*	
S.No.	*Item*	*B* %	*G* %	*B* %	*G* %	*B* %	*G* %	*B* %	*G* %
1.	Failure	42.4	42.0	--	--	50.0	41.0		
2.	Being punished by God	30.4	37.0	31.0	32.0	47.0	51.0	24.0	28.0
3.	Loss of loved one	26.4	28.0	44.0	53.0	44.0	37.0	35.0	68.0
4.	Being seen unclothed	25.6	37.0	25.0	43.0	35.8	39.0		38.0
5.	Hurtig others	24.8	--	--	--	23.1	--		34.0
6.	Thoughts of suicide	23.2	29.0	21.0	--	32.8	31.0	18.0	
7.	Ghosts	21.6	36.0	-	--	--	31.0		

(Contd.)

Table 4.31 : (Contd.)

S.No.	Item	12 Years				14 Years			
		Indian		British		Indian		British	
		B %	G %	B %	G %	B %	G %	B %	G %
8.	Dead people	21.6	32.0	27.0	35.0	23.1	29.0	--	33.0
9.	Heart missing a beat	20.0	28.0	--	--	--	31.0	--	--
10.	Unemployment	19.2	--	18.0	--	44.8	--	23.0	--
11.	Thoughts of being mentally ill	17.6	--	29.0	41.0	--	--	24.0	39.0
12.	Being ugly	16.8	28.0	16.0	34.0	21.6	--	17.0	--
13.	Feeling rejected by others	16.8	--	--	--	23.1	--	--	29.0
14.	Drugs	--	--	24.0	42.0	--	--	15.0	32.0
15.	Thoughts of having a defective child	--	28.0	23.0	52.0	--	38.0	28.0	39.0
16.	Prospect of a surgical operation	--	--	20.0	--	--	--	14.0	--
17.	Dentists	--	--	20.0	--	--	--	--	--
18.	Witnessing surgical operations	--	--	15.0	34.0	--	--	14.0	--
19.	Being alone	--	38.0	--	--	--	--	--	--
20.	Buildings where some-one has died	--	34.0	--	--	--	29.0	--	--
21.	Living away from family	--	33.0	--	--	--	31.0	--	--
22.	Germs	--	30.0	--	--	--	--	--	--
23.	Thoughts of being sexually assaulted	--	--	--	56.0	--	31.0	16.0	55.0
24.	Giving off an offen-sive odour	--	--	--	33.0	--	--	--	34.0
25.	Mice or rats	--	--	--	33.0	--	--	--	40.0
26.	Leaving the inflamm-able gas on	--	--	--	--	24.5	29.0	--	28.0
27.	Being dominated by others	--	--	--	--	24.6	--	--	--
28.	Speaking in public	--	--	--	--	--	--	16.0	--
29.	Going in to dark theatre	--	--	--	--	--	29.0	--	--

Note : In some columns the items are more than 12 because of more than one item sharing a rank.

Table 4.32 : Top Twelve Fears of Adolescents by Age Group

	12 years boys	*%age*	*14 years boys*	*%age*
1.	Loss of loved one	35.2	Loss of loved one	39.1
2.	Being punished by God	30.8	Being punnished by God	34.3
3.	Failure	26.4	Unemployment	32.6
4.	Being seen unclothed	25.2	Failure	29.6
5.	Dead people	24.4	Thoughts of suicide	24.5
6.	Thoughts of being mentally ill	23.2	Being seen unclothed	21.8
7.	Thoughts of suicide	22.0	Thoughts of having a defective child	21.4
8.	Thought of having a defective child	19.2	Thoughts of being mentally ill	20.1
9.	Unemployment	18.8	Being ugly	19.1
10.	Beig ugly	16.4	Feeling rejected by others	17.0
11.	The heart missing a beat	16.0	Leaving inflammable gas on	16.7
12.	Prospect of surgical operation	15.6	Dead people	16.7
13.	Drugs	15.6	Giving off an offensive odour	16.7

Table 4.33 : Top Twelve Fears of Adolescents by Age Group

	12 Years Girls	*%age*	*14 Years Girls*	*%age*
1.	Thoughts of being sexually assaulted	40.6	Loss of loved one	52.5
2.	Loss of loved one	40.6	Thoughts of being sexually assaulted	43.0
3.	Thoughts of having a defective child	39.8	Being punished by God	39.5
4.	Being seen unclothed	39.8	Thought of having a defective child	38.5
5.	Being punished by God	34.3	Being seen unclothed	38.5
6.	Dead people	33.2	Dead people	31.0

(Contd.)

Table 4.33 : (Contd.)

	12 Years Girls	*%age*	*14 Years Girls*	*%age*
7.	Being ugly	30.8	Thoughts of suicide	31.0
8.	Thoughts of suicide	30.0	Hurting others	28.0
9.	Buildings where some-one has died	29.6	Leaving inflammable gas on	28.0
10.	Witnessing surgical operations	28.9	Giving off an offensive odour	26.0
11.	Drugs	27.3	Drugs	26.0
12.	The heart missing a beat	26.9	Pregnancy	25.0
13.	Living away from family	26.9	Mice or rats	20.0
			Witnessing surgical operations	20.0

Table 4.34(a) : Items Feared "Very Much" — Top Twelve Items

Items and Category	*Sample Groups – Male* British Adolescents 12 Yrs. %n-125	British Adolescents 14 Yrs. %n-159	Indian Adolescents 12 Yrs. %n-125	Indian Adolescents 14 Yrs. %n-135
(1)	(2)	(3)	(4)	(5)
I. **Animal**				
Bats	Nil	Nil	Nil	Nil
Mice/Rats	Nil	Nil	Nil	Nil
II. **Classical**				
Being alone	Nil	Nil	Nil	Nil
Fire	Nil	Nil	Nil	Nil
Germs	Nil	Nil	Nil	Nil
Going alone into dark theatre	Nil	Nil	Nil	Nil
III. **Miscellaneous**				
Failure	Nil	Nil	42	50
Making mistakes	Nil	Nil	Nil	Nil
Being punished by God	31	24	30	47

(Contd.)

Table 4.35(a) : (Contd.)

(1)		(2)	(3)	(4)	(5)
Ghosts		Nil	Nil	22	Nil
Thieves		Nil	Nil	Nil	Nil
Unemployment	28%				
IV. **Social Stimuli**					
Speaking in public		Nil	16	Nil	Nil
Feeling rejected by others		Nil	Nil	17	23
Being seen unclothed		25	Nil	26	36
Giving off an offensive odour		Nil	Nil	Nil	Nil
Being dominated by others		Nil	Nil	Nil	25
Loss of loved one		44	35	26	44
Hurting others		Nil	Nil	25	23
Living away from family	28%	Nil	Nil	Nil	Nil
V. **Tissue Damage etc.**					
Open wounds		Nil	Nil	Nil	Nil
Dead people		27	Nil	22	23
Dentists		20	Nil	Nil	Nil
One person bullying another		Nil	Nil	Nil	Nil
Witnessing surgical operations		Nil	14	Nil	Nil
Prospect of a surgical operation		20	14	Nil	Nil
Heart missing a beat		Nil	Nil	20	Nil
Thought of being mentally ill		29	24	18	Nil
Drugs		24	15	Nil	Nil
Being ugly		16	17	17	22
Thoughts of being sexually assaulted		Nil	16	Nil	Nil
Building where someone has died		Nil	Nil	Nil	Nil
Thoughts of suicide		21	18	23	33
Thought of having defective child	44%	23	28	Nil	Nil

Table 4.34(b) : Items Feared "Very Much" — Top Twelve Items

Items and Category		*Sample Groups – Female*			
		British Adolescents		*Indian Adolescents*	
		12 Yrs. %n-130	*14 Yrs. %n-125*	*12 Yrs. %n-126*	*14 Yrs. %n-140*
(1)		(2)	(3)	(4)	(5)
I. **Animal**					
Bats		Nil	Nil	Nil	Nil
Mice/Rats		33	40	Nil	Nil
II. **Classical**	6%				
Being alone		Nil	Nil	38	Nil
Fire		Nil	Nil	Nil	Nil
Germs		Nil	Nil	30	Nil
Going alone into dark theatre		Nil	Nil	Nil	29
III. **Miscellaneous**	6%				
Failure		Nil	Nil	42	41
Making mistakes		Nil	Nil	Nil	Nil
Being punished by God		32	28	37	51
Leaving on inflammable gas		Nil	28	Nil	Nil
Ghosts		Nil	Nil	36	31
Thieves		Nil	Nil	Nil	Nil
Unemployment	15%	Nil	Nil	Nil	Nil
IV. **Social Stimuli**					
Speaking in Public		Nil	Nil	Nil	Nil
Feeling rejected by others		Nil	29	Nil	Nil
Being seen unclothed		43	38	37	39
Giving off an offensive odour		33	34	Nil	Nil
Being dominated by others		Nil	Nil	Nil	Nil
Loss of loved one		53	68	28	37
Hurting others		Nil	34	Nil	Nil

(Contd.)

Table 4.35(b) : Items Feared "Very Much" — Top Twelve Items

(1)		(2)	(3)	(4)	(5)
Living away from family	28%	Nil	Nil	33	31
V. **Tissue Damage etc.**					
Open wounds		Nil	Nil	Nil	Nil
Dead people		35	33	32	29
One person bullying another		Nil	Nil	Nil	Nil
Dentists		Nil	Nil	Nil	Nil
Witnessing surgical operations		34	Nil	Nil	Nil
Prospect of a surgical operaton		Nil	Nil	Nil	Nil
Heart missing a beat		Nil	Nil	28	31
Thoughts of being mentally ill		41	39	Nil	Nil
Drugs		42	32	Nil	Nil
Being ugly		34	Nil	27	Nil
Thoughts of being sexually assaulted		56	55	Nil	31
Building where someone has dead		Nil	Nil	34	29
Thoughts of suicide		Nil	Nil	29	31
Thoughts of having defective child	45%	52	39	28	38

Table 4.35 : Anova Table for Nationality Differences

Sample Group	*F*	*T-Value*	*Level of Significance*
12 Years Boys	1.14	4.60	NS
		8.86	
14 Years Boys	3.10	5.32	NS
		11.26	NS
12 Years Girls	6.67	4.96*	Significant
		10.04	NS
14 Years Girls	0.00098	4.75	NS
		9.33	NS

* 0.05 Level

5

Discussion

This chapter deals with the discussion of the findings of the present study, on fear survey schedule. Three variables are being contrasted in the results presented of this study; namely chronological age, gender differentiation and nationality. Both chronological and gender differences are variables prominent in the studies of adolescent fear described in Chapter 2—Review of Literature. 'Nationality' is not a variable in previous research. This variable nationality provides a cross—cultural distinction, adding new dimension to the study of adolescent fears.

The chapter is divided into three sections.

Section 1	..	Age and Fear
Section 2	..	Gender and Fear
Section 3	..	Nationality and Fear

Section—1

Age and Fear

There is a great deal of conflicting evidence regarding the effect of age on fears of children and adolescents. It was found certain fears declining with age and some others increasing with age, as it was mentioned in Chapter 2. Hall (1897) found that fears of bodily harm and death increase beyond the 6th year Until the end of pubescence. Fear of the dark was noted by Lapouse and Monk (1909) to decline between the ages of 6 and 12 years, but Hall found an increase during pubescence with a decline in adulthood. There is a partial conflict of evidence in relation to 'fear of imaginary creatures' and 'threat of injury'. If we take 'fear of imaginary creatures' to include 'ghosts', then Hall (1897) found this fear increasing until the end of pubescence, but Jersild and Holmes (1935) noted a decrease between 5 and 12 years.

From the findings of the present investigation it would be seen that the age differences were not significant in all the sample groups except in Indian boys where older children were found to have higher fear score compared to younger children. The hypothesis that younger children are likely found to have higher fear score was found to be disproved in this study. On the contrary 14 years old Indian boys have scored significantly higher phobic and total fear scores than 12 years old Indian boys. However this age differences is not noted with other sample groups compared. There were not significant age differences were observed either in Indian girls or British girls and boys groups of 12 years old and 14 years old age groups. These findings are in line with studies conducted earlier by Jersild and Holmes (1935) and Lapouse and Monk (1959).

When means of individual items on Fear Survey schedule were compared (Chapter 4 Section 4) it was observed that except in 12 years old British boys, all other three 14 years age groups had more number of fear items scoring significantly higher mean scores than 12 years age groups. This clearly indicates that number of fears are increasing with the age.

Means (1936) found that both in the number and intensity, fears increased as intelligence decline. The present study revealed the opposite trends as the 14 yrs old girls and boys scored significantly higher mean scores both on total fear score and intelligence score, than 12 years old sample groups. This relationship however was not confirmed in a study by Gastwirth and Silverbratt (1934).

When fear items ranked in the top twelve places and compared by age groups items in the Wolpe/Lang category of 'social stimuli' and 'tissue damage' predominate through both age levels in all sample groups. Similar findings were found by Bamber (1977) and Hall (1897).

Why should items in the 'tissue damage' and 'social stimuli' categories receive greater in frequency and strength through adolescence? 'Tissue damage' fears in top twelve include items such as 'Dead people' 'Thoughts of being mentally ill, 'thoughts of suicide', 'thoughts of having a defective child,' 'being ugly'. This heart missing a beat, 'prospect of surgical operation', 'drugs', thoughts of being sexually assaulted, buildings where someone has died' and 'witnessing surgical operations', there items take us right to the heart of the debate between followers of the psychoanolytical theory and adherents of learning theory in the context of phobias. The learning theory approach, as Rachman (1968) states it, argues that any neutral stimulus, simple or complex, that makes an impact on an individual at about the time that fear reaction is evoked, acquires the ability to evoke fear subsequently.

Fear of 'Witnessing surgical operation' 'prospect of surgical operation' appear in all the sample groups. Having an operation is not universal experience among children. How then could adolescents, come to develop such a strong fear of these items ? They might be acquired by vicarious classical conditioning as explained by Bandura (1965). As a result of listening to adults or other children talk about their own experiences of having an operation, adolescents might have acquired these fears. An alternative explanation is psychoanalytic one. Freud (1970) places fears of operation and bodily mutilation in the category of castration fears which are associated with the phallic phase of development. Fears acquired in childhood continue through adolescence with the same degree of intensity. Blos (1962) says that adolescence is a second edition, of childhood and adolescence have in common the fact that a relatively strong *id.* confronts a relatively weak ago.

The fears evoked by the items of 'dead people' and 'dead animals' fear resemblance to Hebb's (1946) observation of the fear generated in chimpanzees when anesthetized chimpanzees were presented as stimuli. Hebb concluded that it was the lack of responsiveness in a whole animal which determined the fear. This generated incompatible perceptual and intellectual process and hence cerebral disruption of the conflict type.

The 'Social stimuli' items include 'loss of loved one' 'being seen unclothed' Feeling rejected by others' 'Hurting others', giving off an offensive odour'. The Reason for social stimuli items strongly representing among adolescent fears probably centers upon the nature of adolescence itself. Lewin (1961) has argued that the adolescent is in a position similar to what is called in sociology, the 'Marginal man' who stands on the boundary between two groups. The adolescent is a marginal man because he stands on the boundary between children's group and the adult's group. His perceived marginal status leads to shyness, sensitivity and aggressiveness owing to unclearness and instability of ground. His social status is one of conflict (Romala, 1967). Fears regarding man and social relations are prominent for adolescents in studies of Pratt (1945) Angeline and Shedd (1953), Angelno, Dollins and Mech (1966) Gessel, Ilg and Ames (1956) Maurer (1965), while fears regarding bodily integrity and safety are prominent in studies by Pratt (1945) Winker (1949) Angelino and Shedd (1953) and Maurer (1965).

As adolescence it identified as the development stage of 'stress and stain', fears of social stimuli arise due to emotional maladjustment and social immaturity. An outstanding precularity of the teenager as pointed out by Davis (1944) is that it is a time when the individual is attaining physical maturity without necessarily attaining social maturity.

The mean scores of Willoughby neuroticism on three factors namely 'fear of self exposure', and 'liability of mood and inadequacy' increased with age only in case of Indian girls. The difference within the remaining three groups were not significant. This increase with age in neuroticism mean scores for 14 years. Old Indian girls noted on Willoughby neuroticism is not reflected in the neuroticism measured by Junior Eysenck personality questionnaire. This trend of increasing with age is also observed both in boys and girls on psychoticism. On extroversion the age trends are not observed.

The correlation coefficients obtained between probic score and neuroticism were positive and significant in all the sample groups. The same relation was also observed in a study by Bamber (1974). There were no age differences noted. Negative correlation was noted between extroversion and neuroticism on willoughby neurotic schedule.

Though some earlier studies on fear suggested association between the incidence of particular fear and age, there was no continuity of trends through age levels. The present investigation also revealed that the changes number and intensity of fears is not consistent with the chronological age.

Age does have an effect on a small groups of specific fear item in relation to their mean fear scores. The overall observation is that there is no definite trend with regard to age and development of fear.

Some fears habituate with age, others exhibit sensitization and for some fears' intensity is uniform across development. Generally, as children grow they lose some of their fears of material things and natural phenomena but develop other fears such as the fear of failure or fear of particular social situations, persons or groups. Adolescents become more concerned with the effect they have on others, with what others think of them, and of being disliked or rejected by others.

In the present investigation it is observed that the fears increase with age, but the magnitude of it varies across categories of fear.

This study confirmed that the total fear responses increase with age. However there are fluctuations in the number and intensity of fears and is not the same uniform pattern.

Section —2

Gender and Fear

The two most prominent findings to emerge from both the review of the literature and from the present investigation are that, overall, girls are more fearful than boys, and that girls have stronger fears of certain fear items than boys.

The first findings, regarding the fearfulness of girls, is observed both in studies which tabulate fears and in studies which employ some form of the fear survey schedule. Why are girls more fearful than boys? Wilson (1967) emprically testing alternative explanations put forward by Manosevity and Lanyon (1965) found that females have higher fear scores either because they find fear survey schedule items more disturbing or because of social conventions which inhibit males, they report fears more honestly than males.

Correlational comparisons between the fear score and other measures as discussed in the results chapter show that individuals who achieve high scores on tests of anxiety emotionality are also have high scores on fear survey schedule. In the present study girls were found to have significantly higher mean scores on certain factors of Willoughby Neuroticism than boys. If we take phobic score derived from the fear survey schedule to represent extremely disturbed reactions to fear survey schedule items, we find that girls, in all sample groups have significantly higher mean phobic scores than boys.

Jones (1933) has pointed out that' Neuroticism or vulnerability to neurosis implies low tolerance for stress whether it be physical as in painful situations'. Thus individuals scoring high on the factor of Neuroticism, because there emotions are liable, strong and easily aroused (Eysenck and Rachman) and because they have a low tolerance for stress, should react in a strongly positively fashion to fear survey schedule items they find unpleasant *i.e.*, categories such item numbers under the schedule column 'very much'. Since each entry in the 'very much' column contributes four points to the total phobic score, we would expect individuals with high neuroticism scores to have high phobic scores. In this study it was found that the girls not only differed significantly on all factors of neuroticism on Willoughby Neuroticism schedule compared to boys but also had high positive correlation between phobic score and Willoughby Neuroticism schedule total score.

Torgersen (1979) found that the twin with the higher phobic fear factor score was the more dependent and displayed the lower self esteem, orally less aggressive and estimate and showed a more neurotic personality structure girls in this study significantly differed from boys reporting higher phobic fears.

Considering the individual items classified according to Wolpe/ Lange, categories, the items on Tissue damage' have more significantly higher scores on girls compared to boys. These items include 'people who seem in same' 'receiving infections' Doctors' 'thoughts of being sexually assaulted' and 'thoughts of having a defective child'. The above findings are confirmed in a study by Bamber (1977).

The important point to be noted about 'Animal fears is their prominence among girls. Croake and Knowk's (1971) study also revealed that females from South eastern states had greater number fears, especially in relation to animals and natural supernatural phenomenon.

It is especially in the area of animal fears that Valentinine's (1950) innate approach appears to be particularly strong. The Jones and Jones (1928) study demonstrated that fear of snakes is maturational in that a definite fear only emerges around the age of four years. Related to fear of animals is the fear of being looked at. Marks (1969) points out that fear of two staring eyes ubuiquitous throughout the animal kingdom including man. This might go some way to account for the fear of such animals as lions and tigers. Valentine further explains that fears of animals may be a specific instance of the more general moment in objects.

Among the top twelve phobic fears reported, girls and boys shared most of the items in common, except in the few items. 'Fear of unemployment' and 'Feeling rejected by others' were prominent in boys which girls did not share these items with boys. Girls reported fears of 'Buildings where someone has died' and 'witnessing surgical operation' which were not reported by boys.

A positive correlation found between total fear score and total Willoughby Neuroticism schedule score in girls indicate that those who had higher fear scores were also neurotic. Further this finding is also confirmed in the results of Junior Eysenck personality questionnaire that fear score is positively correlated with the neuroticism factor of Junior Eysenck personality questionnaire.

Section—3

Nationality and Fear

The present investigation took 'nationality' as one of the three variables on which data was examined and compared. It is a variable which embrances differences in places of living, race, religion, parental occupation, socio-economic level, life style, norms, taboos, customs, scientific and technological advancement values, family and educational system, climate and culture in general. Thus despite the fact that the variable 'nationality' is not a straight forward amalgum of these differences, it would appear reasonable to assume that they are sufficiently dominant in the variable to allow comparisons with other studies.

Interesting differences were noted related to the nationality of the adolescents. Indian boys and girls showed significantly higher mean scores on total fear and phobic scores than British boys and girls. Why should Indian adolescents display evidence of greater fearfulness than British adolescents ? The answer is neither simple nor straight; nor can there be any single factor explaining this situation. Political, social, economic, familial, child rearing practices and educational issues are intertwined and all have continued to the adolescents fears.

The Indian youth is changing and he is in conflict with many traditional customs (Romala, 1967). The conflicts lead them to develop various fears and if these conflicts are not resolved, the adolescents live in constant fear and guilt.

Rath (1957) observed that adolescents have imbibed the values of new society, economic advancement and social equality. At the same time they perceive that there are several obstacles to achieve them. This sets in frustration, fear and stress.

Rajguru's (1971) probe into juvenile deliquency revealed that young people were the victims of the cruelties of home which led them towards various crimes especially when they were emotionally distributed by the non-satisfaction of their economic and psychological needs.

Olah *et al* (1984) concluded that culture is the most significant single factor among the main effects of anxiety. In this study Nationality (cultural) differences were noted consistently in all the sample groups when the mean scores of individual items on FSS were compared. In all four sample groups Indian boys and girls revealed greater number of fear items which differed significantly from the fear items of British samples. Considering Wolpe/Lang classification, Indian adolescents have more number of classical fears, while the British adolescents have more number of fear items in tissue damage category.

Phobic fear is one of the greatest threats to mental health. The most outstanding feature of top twelve phobic fears in relation to nationality variation within sample groups is that there are more number of items on FSS shared than unique, across two nations. British girls reported fear of animals which Indian groups omit it. Similarly Indian girls reports fears of classical type (fear of being alone, germs, going into dark theatre) while British girls do not show any differences in the percentage of miscellaneous, social stimuli and tissue damage fears. In miscellaneous category there is prominent difference for Indian adolescents in fears of 'failure', 'ghosts' and unemployment.

Fear of failure appear on the top twelve fears of all Indian sample groups. The distribution of this fear would suggest that it is related to anxieties regarding achievement of personal and family goals of many. The problem of educated unemployed has become alarming in India.

To quote Rao, V. K. R. V. "Unemployment hangs like a black shadow over the student world when they complete their studies, there is an uneasy feeling that extra merit considerations play for too important part in recruitment'. Indian adolescents particularly boys are expected to bear much responsibility for the family finances and they face much anxiety and frustration in seeking employment. The percentage of 14 years old Indian boys who reported fear of 'unemployment' is higher as compared with British boys. The despair of an educated unemployed person in Indian is deepened as he has to choose from number of comparative occupational choices and also with a greater competition than before. Another explanation might be that incentives to gain higher standard of living have now spread more widely through mass communications and advertising.

A great deal of fear centres around the work world in India and if the rising standard of living does not keep up with the rising standard of aspirations, then fears will increase. Added to the economic insecurity many young people have the feeling of loss of prestige in not living up to parents expectations. In a country like India in which the new urban occupational opportunities have not caught up with the expansion of the educational system, it is impossible to get jobs commensurate with their abilities of young. Much fear and frustration will therefore be generated until the occupational openings are more in the line with the number of trained personnel for these positions.

Fear of failure and 'thoughts of suicide' appear in the top twelve fears of Indian boys and girls. Failure of children in their school examination is treated or viewed severally by parents especially in case of sons. Ross (1961) pointed out that a good deal of pressures was often put on sons to study and this might take a subtle from such as the expression of keen disappointment or sorrow when son did not pass examination. Disappointment at the failure of a son might take the form of physical punishment such as canning, but the usual form is that of remonstration and constant nagging comparing him with sons of others, which might lead to fears such as 'thoughts of suicide.' This kind of nagging mostly by fathers is so extreme that it appeared to have boomering effect crippling the adolescent's ability to study (Ross 1961). A good deal of fear for adolescents to do well at school and college is due to the belief that their success will reflect back on the family and eventually improve their standard of living. Girls are not an exception to this, in modern India, as there is an increasing trend in girls to come out successfully and take gainful employment outside home to meet the financial pressures. It may be that in a society in which children are expected in support their parents in their old age and help relatives in trouble that more pressure is unconsciously put on adolescents.

Fears of 'feeling rejected' by others and 'hurting others' are reported by all Indian boys. These fears could be explained in terms of adolescent marginality, social sensitivity and child rearing methods followed in training the Indian children. Rejection by parents in associated with a larger number of fears in their children (Sidana and Sinha, 1973), Davitz (1958) in a comprehensive survey of research concerned with behaviour of children, says that punishment and rejection give rise to fear, fear promotes defence reaction and defensive reactions elicit further punishment. In a study conducted by Faizunniasa and Parmeshwaran (1967) it has been found that mother's punishing and rejecting behaviours had more consistent association with children's behavioural problems of difference types.

Rajguru (1971) observed that Indian adolescents experience a more or less ideologies and styles of living to which his attitudes and values are at conflict.

Fear of 'ghosts' and 'building where someone has died' among Indian girls have its origin in the belief of evil spirits or 'demons'. The night is believed to be haunted by ghosts (preta, buta) and naked spirits of those who had died violent deaths and for whom 'Sradha' has not been performed. For ten dyes after cremation, libation of water were poured for the dead and offerings of rice ball (Pinda) and vessels of milk are made for him. On death a man's soul becomes a miserable ghosts unable to pass on to the world of the Fathers or to a new birth and liable to do harm to the surviving relatives. With the performance of the last 'antyesri' rite on the 10th day it acquires a subtle body with which to continue its journey speeded on its way and nourished in the after life with the 'Pindas' offered at periodical 'Sradha' ceremonies. These spirits are considered very dangerous practically to their own surveyors and relatives. Usually the buildings where people have died are the places of fright as they are associated with evil spirits or ghosts. The superstitions is that the souls of dead people who were not satisfied. While living do not leave the dwellings of dear and near and they appear in unusual forms to tease or please the living till they take another birth (Bhashan L.S. 1985).

Fear of 'living away from family' is shared by all Indian girls. It might reflect the social life of girls which is largely confined to their families and relatives. Girls in general lead a sheltered life in Indian society and the idea of leaving the parents home cause certain anxiety in them which calls for new adjustment and contact with much wider social world. While trying out new technique of behaviour which fits into larger social world, the adolescent girls prefer to remain in the security of family. The younger girls who glaze a new trail, will have anxious movements once they leave parents home either for higher education or marriage. The change from intimate larger family unit to the impersonal social world calls for the social skills which would help them to develop a group of supporting friends.

Fears of 'thoughts of being sexually assaulted', 'thoughts of being mentally ill,' 'drugs', witnessing, surgical operation' and 'being ugly' were the phobic fears of British girls and boys which are unique and not expressed by Indian adolescents. These fears mainly reflect the cultural variations of the adolescents. Fear of 'thoughts of being sexually assaulted' which was reported by British adolescents, especially girls might be viewed in terms of sexual permissiveness, opportunities for social interaction and lack of protection by family. Fears of this kind (Physical assault and fear of being with a member of opposite sex) were also reported by the boys and girls in an investigation by Doughlas *et al* (1969).

Mental illness is considered as a serious social evil and problem of western society. It is not surprising to note the fear of 'thoughts of being mentally ill' among the British sample groups. Psychiatric problems are relatively more prevalent in western countries. The most advanced the society is, the more discomfort it gives to the children.

Cultural similarities were also found with the fears of 'being punished by god' Being seen unclothed' 'Loss of loved on' thoughts of suicide 'Dead people' 'Unemployment' and thought of having a defective child'. These are the phobic fears of both the Indian and British adolescents.

Fear of 'Loss of loved one' takes first rank in the phobic fears (50.4) for British adolescents, where as it takes fourth place (34%) for

Indian adolescents. Loss of loved one could mean only death of loved one for Indians. It might indicate separation from the loved spouse as in case of divorce, separation from a close loved person due to broken family or death in the western context.

Fears of 'thought of having a defective child' is experience by 32.2% of British adolescents as against 23.87% of Indian adolescents. Congenital disorders are found to be in increasing trend in Britain. The adolescents seem to be more aware of the consequences of these disorders.

The percentage of phobic fear of 'Being punished by God' is in higher percentage (41.4%) in Indian adolescents than in British adolescents (29.3%) perhaps Indian girls and boys are more aware of the religious value in the training and importance attached to the religious practices by the family.

British adolescents revealed significantly higher scores on neuroticism as measured by Willoughby Neuroticism schedule. Wolpe (1958) regards high scores on neuroticism as persistent unadaptive anxieties reactions which relate mainly to common types of social situations. Does this indicate neurotic personality of British adolescents? Perhaps, they are more inhibitive and reserved in their expressions, than Indian who are specific and frank in expressing their fears.

As discussed in the (Chapter 1) introduction, the nature and meaning of 'fear' and anxiety, the findings of this study clearly indicate that British adolescents are more neurotic and anxious and Indian adolescents are more fearful.

British adolescents were found to be more extroverted and neurotic than Indian adolescents. In line with these findings Anmanth's (1972) revealed that Indians had significantly lower scores on neuroticism and extroversion than Canadians. He attributed that anxieties in Canadians arise partly from the frustration or non-fulfilment of love and belongingness needs. On the other hand in a society like India where majority people worried about bare necessities of life, the anxieties may have an economic source. The differences were also noted by Bamber (1973) utilizing Junior PEN Inventory in which both boys and girls from secondary schools had significantly larger means on neuroticism than grammar school pupils and lower scores for grammar girls on extroversion.

According to Eysenck and Eysenck (1964) a high 'P' scores is described as being solitary, not caring for people troublesome, not fitting in anywhere, hostile and aggressive. In the present investigation Indians scored higher on psychotism and lie score.

A positive correlation was observed between phobic score and neuroticism and fear score and neuroticism. This amounts to indicate that greater the fear, in the adolescents, greater is the neuroticism. These results are further supported by the findings of Bamber (1974)

6
Summary and Conclusion

Fear is one of the most powerful negative human emotions, though we find it to be a constructive emotion for socialization of a child in the formative years of life. Fear takes the possession of human personality. If fear is dropped, the individual blossoms into flowering personality.

The present study has attempted to assess the extent and degree of fears among a normal adolescent population. For the purpose of this study 'fear' has been defined as the positive reaction an individual makes to a verbal stimulus on a questionnaire when he is asked to pick out those items which he thinks he might find frightening. The strength of this fear, as experienced by the individual is determined according to whether he records as having the fear a little, a fair amount, much or very much. Given the information which this investigation has collected regarding the extent and degree of fears as defined above, what value and practical relevance can be derived from it? Two of the answers given (Chapter 1) were (a) that psychiatric judgements require the backing up of normative studies and (b) that a relevant curriculum requires to touch upon the learner's affective concern.

Mayer and Chesser (1970) have pointed out that the irrational fears of normal people differ mainly from the phobias of patients seeking, treatment in that they are less intense and do not sufficiently restrict their activities to interfere with ordinary life. It is also noted by Meyer and Chesser that phobia may result from the absence of appropriate responses due to lack of suitable learning rather than the disruptive effect of anxiety. Thus lack of social skills or of the ability to be appropriately assertive, for example, may be the underlying basis of situational phobias.

One of the goals of epidemiological research is to identify groups who are at risk. If groups who are more likely to develop intense fears can be identified, and if they could received training in making appropriate responses to those objects and situations most likely to produce intense fear reactions, then a reduction in the possible emergence of phobias might be brought about. However, as Marks (1969) has pointed out, little is yet known about the prevalence of phobic disorders in the general adult community. The present study has confirmed previous research that girls are more fearful than boys, and to a lesser extend that Indian adolescents are more fearful than British adolescents. Thus, accepting the hypothesis II (a) and (b).

The hypothesis I (a), and (b) and III (a), that younger children are likely to have high fear score (compared to older children) and the younger children will have significantly higher score on factor of neuroticism compared to older children are rejected in this study as they are disproved.

The hypothesis I (c) that there will be correlation between the fear score and neuroticism score is accepted in this investigation as the correlation between fear score and WNS total score is. The hypothesis framed is proved and accepted. If we hypothesize that more fearful groups are more likely to develop intense fears or phobias, then such groups could be regarded as being 'at risk' with reference to phobias. That females are an 'at risk' population, in the present context, receive support in a study by Marks and Gelder (1966) and Bamber (1974). The hypothesis III (b) that there is likely to be significant difference in the top twelve phobic fears between age groups is not accepted as there is significant difference only in one sample group where 14 years Indian boys showed higher fear score. Significant gender and nationality differences were noted in top twelve phobic fears of adolescent thus accepting the hypothesis.

No studies appear to have reported the incidence of fears or phobias among Indian adolescents as apposed to British adolescents but if we are correct in maintaining that the 'at risk' position of Indian adolescents is analogous to that of girls, then we would expect further research to show that the incidence of fears and phobias among Indian adolescents is higher than that among British adolescents.

Two educational implications appear to arise from the present argument. If girls and Indian adolescents constitute 'at risk' populations with regard to fear and phobias, and if training in the relevant response and the ability to be appropriately assertive could hinder the development of fears and phobias, then such training should constitute part of the 'personal development' curriculum in school, for the 'at risk' groups.

Counselling services for parents, teachers and adolescents help a long way in dealing with fearful and phobic adolescents. Counselling centres with psychologists and psychiatrists should be established. Every school should have an access to such counselling service centres. Parents and 'teachers should be guided to seek help from psychologist and psychiatrist for children suffering from phobias.

Parental attitudes in child rearing play a crucial role in developing children's fears. It was proved beyond doubt that rigid disciplinary practices, rejection and over protection of children result in development of fears in them. Children brought up in an environment of fear, restriction and rigid attitudes develop fears and phobias. Indian child is under pressure in the home environment also constantly, hopped by parents what 'not to do' than 'what to do'. There are more 'don'ts' than 'dos' in his life. As a result, there is more scope for him to develop fears. Non-confirmation to traditional beliefs, norms, sentiments, ideologies and values lead to guilt, conflict and fear in adolescents.

There are more social constraints of fear. The adults have more constraints which are reflected in their communication with their children thus leading to development of fears in them. Thus favourable parental attitudes and child rearing practices avoid the development of fears in children.

Helping adolescents to develop appropriate skills in combating fears and phobias should constitute pare of school programme. When children are helped to learn to respond to a fearful situation appropriately, their fears are reduced. The children should learn to handle fear provoking situations with suitable responses which do not arise fear and inculcate courage to face them.

School curriculum and teachers attitudes are the most important aspects in dealing with fears and phobias in adolescents. School curriculum should be challenging, but should not induce a fear of failure in them. It should provide more challenges which could afford success and achievement. There should be provision for recreational opportunities in school curriculum. Recreation reduces tension and provides relaxation for adolescents and it has therapeutic value for them. Every school should have adequate recreational facilities for pupils.

The curriculum should also provide suitable vocational guidance and training for pupils. This avoids fear and frustration in them by helping adolescents to select suitable vocation and develop their vocational skills. Vocational guidance and training aid adolescents to combat the phobia of unemployment with which most of the adolescents are suffering. National policy on education 1986 which is based on national curricular frame work has proposed that vocational courses cover 10% of higher secondary students by 1990 and 25% by 1995.

The attitude of teachers is the most important factor in the development of child's personality. Teachers unfavourable attitude which seek rigid disciplinary methods in training the adolescents only provoke them to rebel and also develop fears. Love oriented disciplinary techniques and skilful management of class room situations provide the adolescents with an opportunity for personal development and interest in curricular activities. Giving an opportunity for individual expression is an important factor in the development of adolescents. Unfortunately our schools do not provide this, thus creating only frustration and fear in pupils. Suitable training for teachers and refreshers courses, workshops and seminars arranged from time to time provide scope for teachers to develop and improve their skills in handling the class room situations and pupils. Recognizing the individual needs and helping the adolescents in coping up with their curricular and extra curricular requirements help them to develop a healthy personality and eliminate fears and phobias.

Our educational system itself should undergo a transformation to cater to the needs of adolescents. It should be 'learning oriented' instead of 'goal oriented'. There should be provision for 'segregated schools' for the gifted and talented pupils who are above average in intelligence and creativity. Gifted children need a specially tailored curriculum to satisfy their intellectual and emotional needs. Curriculum that does not suit pupils' interests and needs create only frustration and fear.

The grammar school system and 'segregated schools' in United Kingdom cater to the needs of children with above average intelligence and talent. The experiments with 'National curriculum' (*Hindu*-Sunday 22nd Oct., 1989) are undergoing in United Kingdom to give best education to the children, based on the needs of present day society.

The ultimate aim of education is to equip the child with the most excellent technological proficiency so that he may function with clarity and efficiency in the modern world, and for more important to create the right climate so that the child may develop fully as a complete human being. Education should be socially relevant. To provide such education changes in the educational system should be brought accordingly. Education with freedom from fear should be the motto of any educational system. Perhaps the credo of all teachers should be that good teaching is good psychology.

It is especially in the area of animals fears that Valentinines's (1990) innate approach appears to be particularly strong. The Jones and Jones (1928) study demonstrated that fear of snakes is maturational in that definite fear only emerge around the age of four years. Related to fear of animals is the fear of being looked at. Marks (1969) points out that fear of two staring eyes ubiquitous thoughout the animal kingdom including man. This might go some way to account for the fear of such animals as lions an tigers. Valentine further explains that fears of animal may be specific instance of the more general moment in objects.

Among the top twelve phobic fears reported, girls and boys shared most of the items in common, except in the few items. 'Fear of unemployment' and 'Feeling rejected by others' were prominent in boys which girls did not share these items with boys. Girls reported fears of 'Buildings where some-one has died' and 'witnessing surgical operations' which were not reported by boys.

A positive correlation found between total fearscore and total Willoughby Neuroticism schedule score in girls indicating that those who had higher fear scores were also neurotic. Further this finding is also confirmed in the results of Junior Eysenck personality questionnaire that fear score is positively correlated with the neuroticism factor of Junior Eysenck personality questionnaire.

Bibliography

Agras, S., Sylwester, D., Oliveau, D. The apidemilogy of common fears and phobias. Referred to by: Marks, I.M., *Fears and Phobias*. London. Heinemann Medical Books, 1969.

Olah, A., Goobar, I., Magnusson, D., Karrin, H., and Reddy, N.T. Culture, Age and sex as moderating factors in the approisal of anxiety in the environment. *Reports from the Department of Psychology*. The universitv of Stockholm, Stockholm No. 619, pp. 106-91.

Akutagawa, D. 1956. A study in construct validity of the psychoanalytic concept of latent anxiety and test of a projection distance hypothesis. *Unpublished doctroal dissertation*, University of Pittsburgh.

Alan, D., 1983. Children's fear of Animals. *Jr. of Genetic Psychology*. Vol. 142(2), pp. 313-314.

Alan, D., and Celin, R., 1984. Reported fears of animals among biology and non-biology studies. *Psychological Reports*. Vol. 34 (1) pp.18.

Alan D. 1984. Fears and Understanding of animals in middle childhood. *Jr. of Genetic Psychology*. Vol. 145(1), pp. 143-144.

Amies, P.L, Jelder, M.G., Sharp. P.M. 1983. Social phobia: A comparative clinical study. *British Jr. of Psychiatry*. Vol. 142, pp. 174-179.

Angelio, H., Dolkins, J., Mech, E.V. 1956. Trends in the fears and worries of school children as related to socio-economic status and age. *Jr. of Genet. Psychol.*

Angelino, H. and Shedd, C.L. 1953. Shifts in the context of fears and worries relative to choronological age, *Proc. Oklahoma Acad, Sci.* 34, pp. 180-186.

Ananth, S., 1973. A cross-cultural study of Belongigness, Anxiety, Neuroticism and Extraversion. *ICSSR Research Abastracts Quarterly.* Vol. 1. No. 2.

Anth ony, Kenny (1963). *Actions, Emotion and Will* Chapter 3 pp. 67. New York: Harper Publishing Co. 1965.

Anthony, M and Kevin, C. 1982. Behavioural treatment of 'night fears' in children. Maintenance of improvement of 2½ to 3 years follow-up. *Jr. of consulting and clinical Psychology.* Vol. 50(4), pp. 598-599.

Arlinda, A. and James, P. 1984. A development analysis of mother's reports or normal children's fears. *Jr. of Genetic Psychology.* Vol. 144(2), pp. 165-178.

Bndura, A. 1965. Vicarious processes: a case of no-trial learning. In:Berkowitz L. (ed): *Advances in Experimental Social Psychology.* Academic Press, New York, Vol. II.

Bamber J.H. 1973. Adolescent marginality. A further study *Genetic Psychol, Monogr,* 88, pp. 3-21.

Bamber, J. H. 1977. The factorial structure of adolescent resposes to a fear survey schedule. *The Jr. of Genetic Psychology.* 130, pp. 229-238.

Bamber J.G. 1974. The fears of adolescents. *Jr. of Genet, Psychol.* 25, pp. 127-140.

Bandura, A., Reese, L., and Adams. N. 1982. Microanalysis of action and fear arousal as a function of differential levels of perceived self efficacy. *Jr. of personality and Social Psychology.* Vol. 42(1) 5-21.

Bercz, J.M. 1968. Phobias of childhood: *etiology and treatment psychological Bulletin.* 70(6), 694-720.

Bernstein, D.A. and Allen, G.J. 1969. Fear survey schedule (II): Normative data and factor analysis a large college sample. *Behav. Res. and Therapy.* 7, pp. 403-407.

Bhashan, A.L. 1985. *Wonder that was India*—Calcutta, Rupa & Co.

Blos, P. 1962. *On Adolescents.* The Macmillon Company, NY.

Bowlly, J. 1973. *Separation Anxiety and Anger.* Horgarth Press, London.

Braun, P.R. and Reynolds, D.J. 1969. A factor analysis of a 100-items fear survey inventory. *Behav, Res. and therapy.* 7, pp. 399-402.

Berger, L. and McGaugh, J.L. 1965. Critique and reformaulation of 'Learning theory', approach of Psychotherapy and neurosis. *Phychological Bulletin.* 63(5) pp. 338-358.

Bregman, E.O. 1934. An attempt to modify the emotional attitudes of infants by the conditioned response technique. *Jr. or Genetic, Psychology* 45-169.

Clandette. J. and David. B. 1983. What do our Teenagers fear? *Child Psychology Quarterly.* Vol. 16(1), pp. 1-8.

Croake, J.W. and Knox, F.M. 1971. A second look at adolescent fears. *Adolescents.* 6, pp. 279-284.

Davis, K. 1944. Adolescents and the social structure. *The annals of the American academy of political and social Science.* Vol. 236, pp: 8-15.

Davitz, J.R. 1958. Contributions of research with children to a theory of maladjustment. *Child Development.* 29; pp. 3-7.

Davidson, P.M. White, P.N, Smith, D.J. and Poppen, W.A. Content and intensity of fears in middle childhood rural and urban boys and girls. *Jr. of Genetic, Psychol.* Vol., I 150(I), 51–58, PA. Vol. 76, No. 8, 1989.

Davis, Anna.F., Rosenthial Ted, L. and Kelley, Johh, E.R. (Nemphis state U). 1981. Actual fear cues, prompt therapy and rational enhance participat modelling with adolescents. *Behaviour Therapy.* Vol. 12(4) pp. 536-542.

Doconell and Perez, 1982. Behavioural treatment of "night fears" in children. Maintenance of improvement at 2½ to 3 years follow-up. *Jr. of Consulting and Clinical Psychology,* Vol. 50(4). pp. 598-599.

Despert, J.L., 1946. Anxiety, Phobias, and fears in young children. *Nervous Child.* 5, pp. 8-24.

Derevensky Jeffrey C. 1979. Children's fears. A developmental comparison of normal and exception children. *The J. of Jenetic Psychology.* 135, pp. 11-21.

Dixon, J.H. de Morchauz, C., Sandler, J. 1957. Patterns of anxiety: The phobias. *Brit. J. Med. Psychol.* 30, pp. 34-40.

Drever, J. 1952. *A Dictionary of Psychology*. Harmondrowrth. Pengerin Books.

Duff. R., A comparison of the fears of mildly retarded adults with children of their mental age and chronological age matched controls: *Journal of behaviour therapy and experimental psychology*. Vol. 12(2), 121-124.

Emil. K and Fritz. M. 1981. Kotamnesllsche untersuchungzur statioaren therapic schewere schuphobiien (Inpatient of severs school phobia: A follow-up study). *Zeitchrift furtinder-and Jugendpsychiatre* Vol. 9(3), pp. 273-287.

English, H.B. 1929. Three cases of the 'conditioned fear response'. *Jr. abnorm. Soc. Psychol.* 30,24, pp. 221-225.

English, O.S. and Pearson, G.H.J. 1965. *Emotional problems of living London*: George Allen and Unwin, 3rd Ed.

Eysenck, H.J. and Rachman, I. 1965. *The causes and cure of neurosis.* London: Rolutledge and Kegan Paul.

Eysenck and Rachman. *Manual of the Eysenck Personality Questionnaire* (Junior and Adult) Hodder and Stoughton.

Emil. K. and Fritz. M. 1981. Impatient of severe school phobia: A follow-up study. *Zeitichrift furkinder—and Jugend Psychiatre*. Vol. 9(3), pp. 273-287.

Evans Philip.D. and Garfield. D and Narmon. (North East London Polytechnic, England). 1981. Children's self-initiated approach to spiders. *Behaviour Research and Therapy*, pp. 543-546.

Fazio, A.F. 1969. Verbal and Overt—behavioural assessment of a specific fear. *Jr, Consult, and Clin, Psychol.* 33, pp. 705-709.

Faizunnisa and Parameshwaran, 1957. Social adjustment of a group of early adolescent boys in *J. of Psychological Researches.* Vol. (3).

Farley, F.H., Mealiea, W.L., and Sewell, T.V. 1981. Sex differences, responses sets and response biases in fear assessment. *Jr. of Behaviour therapy and experimental Psychiatry.* Vol. 12 (3) pp. 203-212.

Frank, F.H., Sewell T.V. and Meallia, W.L. (1982). Sex differences in medial fears of college students. *College Student Journal.* Vol. 16(3) pp. 202-204.

Feshback, S. and Feshback, N. 1963. Influence of the stimulus object upon the complementary and supplementary projection of fear. *J. abnorm. Soc. Psychol.* 66(5) pp. 498-502.

Freud, A. 1970. the symptomatiology of childhood. *Psychoanlaytic study of the child.* 25, pp. 19-44.

Freud, S. 1933. A phobia in a five year old boy. *Collected Papers.* Hogarth Press. London. Vol. III.

Freud, S. *Inhibitions, symptoms and anxiety.* The Hogarth Press. London, 1961.

Garssen, Veenendoal and Bloemink, 1983. Agoraphobia and the hyperventialization syndrome. *Behav. Res. Ther.* Vol. 21, No. 6, pp. 643-649.

Geer. J.H. 1965. The development of a scale of measure fear. *Behav. Res. Therapy,* 3, pp. 45-53.

Gero, G. 1955. *Defense in symptom formation, year of Psychoanalysis.* 10, pp. 113-127.

Gesell, A., Ilg, F.L. Ames, L.B. 1956. *Youth: The years from the ten to sixteen.* Hamish Hamilton, London.

Gibson, E.J. and Walk, R.D. 1960. *The Visual Cliff.* Scientific American.

Grossberg, J.M. and Wilson, H.K. 1965. A correlational comparsion of the Wolpe—Lang Fear Survey schedule and Taylor Manifest Anxiety scale. *Behav. Res. and Therpay,* 3, pp. 125-128.

Hall, G.S. 1897. A study of fear. *American J. of Psychol.,* 8(2), pp. 147-249.

Hebb, D.O. 1946. On the nature of fear. *Psychological Review.* 53, pp. 259-276.

HEIM.A.W., 1970. *Manual for the AH_4 group test of general intelligence.* NFER Publishing Company Ltd. pp. 1-16.

Hicks, J.A. and Hayes, M. 1938. Study of the characteristics of 250 Junior High School Children. *Child. Dey.* 9, pp. 219-242.

Hurlock, E.B. 1949. *Adolescent development.* McGraw-Hill, New York.

James, F Jones, G.E. and Dickson. A.L. 1983. Modified desensitization approach for the treatment of phobic behaviours in children. A quas: experimental case study *Jr. of clinical child, psychology.* Vol. 12(2), pp. 198-201.

Jamie and Theresa, M. 1984. Fear of animals What is prepared? *British Jr. of Psychology.* Vol. 75(1), pp. 37-42.

Jersild, A.J. 1960. *Child Psychology,* Staple Press. London 5th Ed.

Jersild, A.J. and Holmes, F.B. 1935. Children's fears. *Child Development Monographs,* 20.

Jones, H.E. and Jones, M.C. 1928. A study of fear. *Childood Edu.* 5, pp. 136-143.

Jones, M.C. 1993. Emotional development. In : Murchison, C. *A Handbook of child psychology.* Clark Unviersity, Worscester. Vol. I.

John, C. and Jack. C. 1983. Study of fears of elementary school children. *Elementary School Guidance and Counselling.* Vol. 18(2) pp. 82-87.

Joanne, and Glenn. 1984. Children's fear responses to small media: Testing some plagetian predictions. *Journal of communication.* Vol. 34(2), pp. 90-103.

Kathellen. A. 1985. A fears and worries of young children as expressed on a contertual play setting. *Jr. of Child Psychology and Psychiatry and Allied Discipline.* Vol. 26(6) pp. 981-987.

Klopf, Donald and Cambra, Ronald, 1980. Appression about speaking among college students in the Phillippiness. *Perceptual and Motor skills.* Vol. 51(3 p + 2) pp. 12.

Kureshi, Afyal and Khan, Rahat. A. 1981. Fear of failure motivation as related to certain social variables. *Journal of Psychological Research* Vol. 25 (2), pp. 89-93.

Kartsounis, C.D. and Pickersgill, Maxy J. 1981. Orienting responses to stimuli. Others fears *British Journal of Clinical Psychology,* Vol. 20(4) pp. 261-273.

Kazuhiko, A. 1981. (U of Occupational and Environmental Health, School of Medicine, Kitakyushu, Japan). Age—sex trends of phobic and anxiety symptoms in adolescents. *British Jr. of Psychiatry.* Vol. 138, pp. 297-302.

Klingman. A and Ezra. W. 1982. The relationship of proximity to tension areas and size of settlement of fear levels of Israli. *Children Jr. of behaviour therapy and experimental Psychiatry.* (Vol. 13(4), pp. 312-323.

Kartdsounis, L.D. Mervyn Smith. J. and Rickersg Ill mary. J. 1983. Factor analysis of the responses of British University students to the fear survey schedule (ESS-III). *Personality and individual differences.* Vol. 4(2), pp. 157-163.

Klingman, A and Ezra W. (1983). Analysis of Israeli Childrens Fears: *A comparison of religions and secular communities.*

Landy, E.J. and Gaupp, L.A. 1971. A factor analysis of the fear survey schedule. III. *Behav. Res. and Therapy* 9, pp. 89-93.

Lang. P.J. 1969. 122 item fear survey schedule referred to by: Rubin, S.E. and Lawlis, G.F.: Factor analysis of the 122 item fear survey scheudule. *Behav. Res. and Therapy.* 7, pp. 381-386.

Laynon, R.J. and Manosavitz, M. 1966. Validity of self-reported fear. *Behav. Res. & Therapy* 4, pp. 259-263.

Lapouse, R. and Mons. M.A. 1959. Fears and Worries in a representative sample of children. *Amer. J. Orthopsychiat.* 29, pp. 803-818.

Lawlis, G.F. 1971. Response styles of a patient population on the fear survey schedule. *Behav. Res. and Therapy.* pp. 95-102.

Lief, N.J. 1967. Anxiety reaction. In: Freedman, A. M. and Kalpan, H.I. (Eds): *Comprehensive textbook of Psychiatry*, Williams and Wilkins. Maltimore.

Lanzetta. J.T. and Ors. Scott P. 1981. (Dartmouth Coll) Stimulus properties of facila expressions and their influence on the classifical conditioning of fear. *Motiation and Emotion.* Vol. 5(3). pp. 225-234.

Landis. A. 1964. In: *marks, I.M. Fears and phobias.* London. Heinemenn. 1969.

Liddell. H.S. 1950. The role of vigilence in the development of animal neurosisi, J. Junin Eds. *Anxiety*, New York, Grune and Strnattin, pp. 83-96.

Lewis 1969. In Spielberger C.D. and Surason. I.G. *Stress and Anxiety* Vol. (I) John Wiley and Sons 1975.

Lewin. C. and Williams, R.J. Fears of Aids. 1989. The impact of public anxiety in young people. *British Journal of Psychiatry*. Vol. 253. 833-824. PA Vol. 76. No. 8, 1989.

Maofarlane, J.W. Allen, L. Honzik, M.P. 1954. *A development study of the behaviour problems of normal children between 2 montsh and 14 years.* University of California Press, Berkeley.

Manosevitz, M, and Lanyon, R.I. 1965. Fear survey schedule a normative study. *Psychol. Rep.* 17 pp. 699-703.

Marks, I.M. ans Gelder, M.G. 1966. Different ages of onset in varieties of phobia. *Amer. J. Psychiat* 123(2) 218-221.

Marks, I.M. and Herst, E. 1969. The open door: a survey of agoraphobics in Britain. Referred to by: Marks. I.M. *Fears and Phobias.* Heinemann Medical Books, London.

Maurer, A. 1965. What children fear. *J. Genetic Psychol.* 106, pp. 265-277.

May, R. 1950. *The meaning of anxiety.* The Ronald Press Co., New York.

Mary. A. and Margaret, R. 1981. An application of a group counselling technique with school phobic adolescents. *Adolescence.* WIN. Vol. 16(64) pp. 901-904.

Means, M.N. 1936. Fears of one thousand college women. *J. abnorm. Soc. Psychol.* 1, pp. 291-311.

Morgan, G.A and Ricciuti, H.N. 1967. Infant's responses to stranger during the first year. In: Foss, B.M. (Ed.): *Determinants of infants behaviour*, London, Methuen.

Ost. L.G. and Hugdhal. K. 1983. Acquisition of A Goraphobia. Mode of onset and anxiety response patterns. *Behav. Res.* Vol. 21, No. 6, pp. 623-631.

Prasad A. Sarma P. and Rao S. (1974) in Buch, M B. *A Survey of research in education*, Centre of Advanced studies in Education, The M. S. University of Baroda, 1974.

Pfister, O. 1948. *Christianity and fear.* George Allen and Unwin Ltd.

Punamaki R.L. 1982. *War and Psychological Research*, (Finn) *Psykologia*, Vol. 17(1), pp. 3-11.

Por Hock, 1950. *Anxiety*. New York Green and getration pp. 183-196.

Pikunas, J. and Clary, J. 1962. Fears in normal and emotionally deisturbed children. *J. Psychol. Studies* 13, pp. 159-164.

Pratt, K.C. 1945. A study of the 'fears' of the rural children. *J. Genetic Psychol*, 67, pp. 179-194.

Rachman, S. 1968. *Phobias: Their nature and control springfield*. Charles C. Thams.

Rado, S. 1964. Emergency behaviour. In buch. P.H, and Zubin J. (Eds.): *Anxiety*. Hafner Publishing Co., New York.

Rath, 1971. In Buch M.B.A. *A survey of research in education*. Center of Advanced study in Education. The M.S. University of Baroda, 1974.

Rajgury, 1971. In; Buch, M.B. *A survery of research of education*. Center of Advanced study in education. The M.S. University of Baroda, 1974.

Rao. U.K.R.V. 1968. Problem of student unrest. *In youth in ferment* Ed. Gupta R.C. pp. 11-17.

Ross. A. 1961. *The Hindu famly in its urban setting*. Oxford University Press.

Riger, S. *et al* 1981. Community ties and urbanities fear of Crime. An ecological investigation. *American journal of community psychology* Vol. 9 (6). pp. 653-665.

Richard J.R. and Blains W.D. 1983. A developmental genetic analysis of common fears from early adolescence to early adulthood *Child Development*. Vol. 54(2), pp 361-368.

Rachman, J. 1978. *Fear and Courage*. W.H. Freeman and Company, San-Francisco.

Rachman. 1968. *Phobias: Their nature and control*. Charles C. Thomas. Springfield.

Rothstein, W. Holmes, G.R. Boblitt, W.E. 1972. A factor analysis of the fear survey schedule with a Psychiatric population. *J. Clin. Psychol.* 28, pp. 78-80.

Rubin, B.M. Katkin, E.S. Weiss, B.W. 1968. Factor analysis of a fear survey schedule. *Behav. Res. and Therapy*, 6, pp. 65-75.

Rubin, I.E. Lawlis, G.F. Tasto, D.L. Namebek. I. 1969. Factor analysis of the 122 item fear survey schedule. *Behav. Res. and Therapy.* 7, pp. 381-386.

Romala, 1967. The areas of conflicts between parents and their teenage children. *An unpublished master's thesis.* Sri Venkateswara University, Thirupati.

Schachter, S. and Singer, J.E. 1962. Cognitive, Social and Psychiological determinants of emotional state. *Psychological Review.* 69(5), pp. 379-399.

Scherer, M.W. Nakamura, C.Y. 1968. A fear survey schedule for children (FSS-FC). A factor analytic comparison with manifest anxiety (CMAS). *Behav. Res. and Therapy.* 6, pp. 173-182.

Spiegler, M.D. and Liebert, R.M. 1970. Some correlates of self-reported fear. *Psychological Reports*, 26, pp. 691-695.

Spitz. R. 1965. *The first year of life.* International Universities Press. New York.

Strean, H.S. 1967. A family therapist looks at little Hans. *Family Process.* 6(2), pp. 227-234.

Sidana and Sinha, 1974. Child rearing practices and the development of fears in children. *Indian J. of Psychol.* Vol. 48 Part II, pp. 34-43.

Sidna, V.A. 1967. Comparative study fears in children. *J. of Psychological Research*, 1(1), pp. 1-6.

Smith, P.K. and Micheal Lewis, Leonard, A. Rosenblum 1974. Social and situational determinants of fear in the play group. *Origine of fear.* A Leonard John Willey & Sons.

Sing, Satvir & Lunyal, Kontesh (Gurunank Dev. U. Amritsar, India), 1980. Sex differences. Second order factors among some Psychotic correlates of hostile press measure of fear of failure. *British Journal of 'Projections—Psychology and Personal Study* Vol. 25(2), pp. 1-6.

Sing, Satvir and Vanvaria, Kiran (Gurunank Dev. U. Amritsar, India), 1980. Structure of irrelations among fear of success, motivation and personality measures. *Asian Journal of Psychology and Education*. Vol. 6(2). pp. 17-75.

Sing, Satvir (Gurunank Dev. U., Amritsar, India), 1981. Fear of failure among females as related to personality, locus of control, behaviuour problems and child rearing practices. *Personality study and groups behaviour*. Vol. 1(2), pp. 96-106.

Sartory, G. *et al* 1987. Return of fear: The role of rehearsal. *Behaviour Research and Therapy*, Vol. 20(2) pp. 123-124.

Saigh, Philip, A. 1982. The Lebanese Fear Inventory; A normative report. *Jr. of clinical Psychology*. Vol. 38(2) pp. 352-255.

Shippee. G.E. *et al.* 1982. Community perceptions of natual disarter and post. disaster mental health services. *Jr. of Community Psychology*. Vol. 10(1), pp. 23-28.

Schachter, S. and Singer J.E. 1962. Cognitive, social and Psychoiological determinants of emotional state, *Psychological Review*, 69(5) pp. 379-399.

Sullivan. 1956. In, spiel berger, C.D. and Sarson I.G. *Stress and Anxiety*. Vol (1) John Wiley and Son's 1975.

Torgarsen. S. 1979. The nature and origin of common phobic fears. *Bri. J. Psychiat.* 134, pp. 343-51.

Timothy, J.O. *et al.* 1981. Desensitization for on severe phobia of fourteen year old male. *Child behavior therapy*. Vol. 3(2-3), pp. 67-78.

Thomas H. *et al* 1985. Fears in Children and adolescents: Normative data. *Behaviour Research and Therpay*. Vol. 23(4), pp. 465-467.

Thomas, W. and Rebecca. S. 1985. Preschool fears. Longtudinal sequences and Cohort changes. *Children Study Journal*. Vol. 15(2), pp. 147-156.

Valentine, C.W. 1950. *The Psychology of early Childhood*. Methuen and Co., London, 4th Ed.

Vanvaria, Kiran, Agrawal, Rita & Singh, Satvir Gurunank Dev. U., Amritsar, India), 1981. Some characteristics of fantasy-based measure of fear of success among males and females. *Indian Journal of Clinical Psychology*. Vol. 8(2), pp. 95-100.